Church Education for Tomorrow

Church Education for Tomorrow

by

WESNER FALLAW

Philadelphia

THE WESTMINSTER PRESS

LIBRARY OF CONGRESS CATALOG CARD NO. 60-9711

PRINTED IN THE UNITED STATES OF AMERICA

To
my daughter Nancy (1952–   )
and
my mother (1882–   )
two pedagogically inclined persons

Contents

Contents

Preface

A FITTING subtitle for this book might be: for harassed churchmen, TRANSMUTATION OF THE SUNDAY SCHOOL AND THE PASTORAL OFFICE; for uneasy Sunday school teachers, THE JOYS OF RELEASE; for fathers and mothers, ON REORDERING YOUR CHILD'S WEEK; and for seminaries and their financial supporters, RESTRUCTURING THEOLOGICAL EDUCATION might not be amiss. To be sure, if there were to be something for everyone, the risk would be incurred of offering too little for anyone — a safely calculated risk, I hope you will soon agree. And who can doubt that Protestants want to see a real possibility of establishing better teaching and learning in the churches?

For some time past I have had opportunity beyond the confines of my teaching community to discuss the proposals that I elaborate here. In lectures, workshops, and conferences with laymen and clergymen there has been examination of the issues raised — and lively exchange. Just how lively would require many pages for the telling. For instance, at a luncheon with a group of national leaders who had just attended one of my lectures, I was greeted with polite inarticulateness — that is, until I expressed regret over lack of discussion. Whereupon, a person whose published and other contributions I have appreciated over the years, said: "Well, what do you *expect* us to say? You're talking us out of our jobs! "

Not necessarily so. And as I shall indicate in Chapter 7, if certain of my proposals were widely adopted, great numbers of people now engaged in ministries at large would be needed in local churches for work that many would account far more significant and satisfying.

Another example: a magazine editor asked for an article, provided I would not "pull the rug out from under the Sunday school." If I am pulling the rug, it is perhaps more of a tug than a jerk, designed to awaken any who may be sleeping on it; for we in the churches might well arouse ourselves and take a stand that will give us more confidence than is now apparent in our teaching. Certainly I have been heartened by correspondents who testify at length to the hope in them evoked by the call for a more valid teaching, by the most capable persons within the Christian community. Ours is a faith to be taught, and taught with all the competency we can summon; hence my position that it is both logically correct and doctrinally permissible for pastors rather than laymen to carry the main responsibility for classroom teaching.

It is yet more encouraging to find that certain pastors over the country are already doing considerable teaching. One pastor writes that he has actually felt guilty about it, so literally has he taken the idea that the pastor is to be a "teacher of teachers." I shall discuss the question of the ministry of the laity, particularly in Chapter 6, and stand ready in person for stout defense of the conviction that there are innumerable church tasks more congenial to laymen than teaching. By drift and neglect the respective responsibilities of laymen and pastors have become obscure, to the discomfort of all. If CHURCH EDUCATION FOR TOMOR-

ROW can bring a bit of illumination to this problem, I shall be gratified. And indeed my purpose is larger than that of clarifying only the educational aspect of church life, as central as that endeavor is to this book.

Although my focus is mainly on the local church, I attempt to show wherein churches and seminaries may affiliate, to the end that theological education shall actually prepare men and women for ministries detailed in these pages. For behind the church stands the seedbed, the seminary; and behind the seminary, lay contributors whose enlarged support is indispensable if pastors are to be trained to meet the whole need of the church today. And by "whole" I have in mind not more tasks for pastors but concentration on the most appropriate tasks. In the main, administration by laymen is both their proper work and a means of freeing pastors for full exercise of their calling, their training and abilities. To this a layman — at a conference of local church leaders — responded, "That's what I've wanted all along!" For how many thousands of Protestants he speaks, I leave to the reader to determine.

I am indebted to all the anonymous persons quoted in this book, and especially to students and others whose appraisal of its content continues to be both constructive and welcome. Through these servants I glimpse the reality of the household of God.

WESNER FALLAW

Newton Centre
Massachusetts

1

From Sunday School to Church Education

PARENTS, Sunday school teachers, pastors, and a good proportion of the public realize that by its very nature the Sunday school is unequal to the responsibility for educating this generation in Christian faith and knowledge. Moreover, official boards and education committees of local churches, along with pupils, sometimes despair of ever having first-rate teaching and learning within Protestantism. Certainly some churches may take justifiable pride in the advance they have made in their educational work, yet it must be acknowledged that many persons suspect that church classes are predominantly dull and ineffectual instruments for guiding the development of pupils and informing them about the nature and meaning of life under God.

If there is validity in the oft-repeated assertion that the products of our churches are religiously illiterate, then we shall be wise to look to our teaching and take necessary steps to correct the prevailing situation in which there is scant — if any — preparation of lessons by pupils or teachers. And well may we ask ourselves: Are boredom and behavior problems, which plague so many Sunday schools, due to human perversity so much as to directionless teaching and low expectations on the part of teacher and pupils?

And why is it that pupils — backed by their parents — almost invariably pass up a session of the church class when other affairs beckon?

But it is not helpful to dwell on the shortcomings of Sunday schools. Anyone can provide his own evidence that they are inadequate for the teaching aspect of Christ's Great Commission to his followers. This volume is written with a twofold objective: (1) that of exploring the meaning of nurture in Christ and (2) that of proposing a teaching program that gives maximum promise of producing informed minds and conduct governed by the same spirit that was in Christ. To this end we shall examine what is involved in first-rate teaching and learning in our churches. More specifically, we shall describe an education aimed at growth in grace and knowledge of our Lord. Seminaries, denominational and interdenominational leaders, and concerned laymen are invited to ponder the significance of the fact that an untold number of Protestant churches are ready for genuine education. The phrase " genuine education " raises two basic questions to which partial answers are given in this chapter. Who should teach? What is better than the Sunday school for providing education by the church? [1]

The individual who is best prepared, or who has the best opportunity for preparing himself, is the one to teach — that is, the pastor. [2] Ordinarily he is well-grounded in Biblical, theological, historical, and other knowledge relevant to Christian faith and understanding. When he combines knowledge with effectiveness in actual teaching his church is blessed. Granted that many or most pastors now are uninterested if not incapable of teaching, they remain the only persons in the churches who have spent sufficient years in acquiring requisite Biblical and theological knowledge. This fact is worthy of contemplation as churches wrestle with the question: Who is qualified to preside over our classrooms?

Provision for lay leadership education, institutes, workshops, conferences, laboratory and demonstration classes has proved unsatisfactory for making lay men and women competent to teach. Despite exceptions, results of teacher-training efforts demonstrate the desirability of the traditional Sunday school's giving place to solid church education offered by pastor-teachers. Amateur lay teaching needs to recede in favor of pastor-teachers, men and women who have earned a seminary degree, or its equivalent, and who have learned to teach under an internship plan as rigorous as any used by leading universities in training teachers for general education.

The qualified church teacher, therefore, is to be thought of as one who knows the Bible, theology, persons and how they learn, and is competent in classroom teaching. Moreover, he looks upon teaching with the same seriousness with which he views preaching, remembering that Jesus alternated between preaching and teaching and commissioned his followers to do both. He also remembers that from its inception Christianity has been a teaching ministry no less than a ministry of proclamation.

Unhappily, differing from Judaism and Romanism, Protestantism has required less competency in teaching than in preaching. And while American churches have become increasingly exacting about preaching and pastoral qualifications, they have coasted along for at least a century and a half without stipulating that teaching qualifications should be just as exacting. Hence, while only certain ones are permitted in a pulpit — to discourse for twenty minutes — almost anyone available is urged to enter a Sunday school room and hold forth for forty minutes. We who expend every effort to see that our children have the best possible public-school teacher do less than is necessary to ensure for them capable church teaching. Such things ought not to be and need no longer be, once we assess the error of our drift and neglect and take the steps necessary for establishing solid church education.

By church education is meant a teaching-learning enterprise grounded in the life of the church and the Christian heritage, and guided by the pastor-teacher as he seeks to help persons experience God in Christ. In order for this education to take effect, the pastor will have to want to teach, and want to do it enough to realign his pastoral duties; seminaries will need to prepare men and women for teaching; and churches will have to transfer most of their teaching from Sunday to weekday hours, thus relying less on released- or dismissed-time plans than on an after-school-hours plan like that long used by Hebrew schools.

Desire to teach means intending to share knowledge and guide the learner's growth by means of entering into an understanding, affectionate, and continuing relationship with him. Not casual and superficial contacts but deep relationships mark the teacher-pupil experience. In the pulpit the preacher gives himself primarily to God and the majesty of divine truth. In the classroom, as in authentic pastoral relations of all kinds, the pastor's focus is on giving himself to the person, and on a jointly shared quest for the meaning of commonplace experiences with respect to ultimate truth. Whatever the giving — whether in pulpit, classroom, or elsewhere — the good shepherd spends himself for the sake of his parishioner-pupil and his need to grow in grace and in knowledge of Christ.

Desire to teach the young means being a pastor to children and adolescents as well as to adults, daring to assume direct responsibility for the learner's faith and conduct. Desire to teach means risk of misguiding youth who, as they draw close to their pastor in the venture of faith and knowledge, tend to identify with him, take their values from him, look at God through his eyes. In some respects, therefore, teaching is a more awful responsibility than preaching, for it invites a more intimate relationship between pastor and pupils.

A review of the status of teaching in the early church, during the Reformation, and in early Calvinistic and Puritan practices, shows that there is precedent for teaching by the parson. Although at this writing unpublished, research by Prof. Robert W. Henderson, of the University of Tulsa, deals with the history of the doctoral (teacher) office from its inception in Geneva (1541) to the debates regarding it in the Westminster Assembly (1643). Contrary to the current emphasis on the pastor's being a "teacher of teachers," there is both historical and doctrinal reason for pastors to undertake direct teaching. Meantime, some pastors are giving renewed attention to teaching church membership classes, often lengthening them to a year's term or more and making of them respectable teaching and learning enterprises. This is certainly a step in the right direction.

The centrality of the sermon in Protestantism has served to cause seminaries to concentrate on preparing men to preach. Little or no attention is directed toward preparing them to teach. Courses in religious education for bachelor of divinity candidates deal mainly with educational theory and problems of organizing and supervising Sunday school and youth programs. Not pastor-teachers but pastor-administrators are envisioned in these courses, but ways can be found to correct this situation, once the task of nurturing persons in Christian faith and conduct is accorded the importance it deserves. When this is done no one less well equipped than a pastor-teacher will be entrusted with church teaching.

Seminary curriculums may well elevate pastoral teaching to the plane occupied by preaching. Seminarians need to be taught age-level capacities of children and youth, together with appropriate materials of instruction. Seminars and tutorials related to intern teaching should feature creativity and guided activities in the work with young children, and the significance of dialogue and conversation as the teacher and older children and youth and adults analyze and probe the meaning of Christian faith and conduct.

Helpful clues for preparing pastors to teach can be found in recent denominational curriculums. For example, the Seabury series (Episcopal), although designed for use by lay teachers, presupposes doctrinal and ecclesiastical knowledge generally mastered only by seminary graduates; hence, it seems more appropriate for use by the latter in teaching children. Emphasis is on the pupil's being Christian now, at his developmental level, rather than on getting ready to live as a Christian at some future time. Teaching procedure starts where pupils are in their interests and problems of living, effects a relationship between teacher and pupils that enables the class to move through present interest into an experience with Christ as he is revealed in Scripture and in his continuing revelation, the life of the church. The teaching process requires great skill and obviously teachers-in-training ought to have much practice under guidance. In Chapters 7 and 8 we shall consider a solution to this problem.

Local churches seeking an educational program superior to the Sunday school may turn to what is here called " church education." Bear in mind that in church education:

1. Not less use but less misuse of laymen is involved in transferring most of the teaching from laymen and the Sunday school hour to the pastor and weekday periods. In the majority of single-pastor churches, in the foreseeable future children up to about ten years of age will continue in the Sunday school. With upper junior age and older children, laymen will be needed to assist the pastor-teacher on weekdays by conducting field trips and interest groups. Furthermore, in most situations lay assistants will likely extend these and other activities into the Sunday school hour for preadolescents, using this opportunity to direct missionary and service projects, choirs, dramatics, and the like.

2. A pastor may teach six to eight hours a week, preferably at afterschool periods, using the best textbooks available and helping each pupil achieve a sense of progression in the course of study. Beyond the teaching of content, the teacher will strive to make of the class a fellowship through which children enter into the life of the redemptive community, the church, the better to live as Christians in the world, serving it according to their abilities.

3. Care is to be exercised in arranging for pastoral teaching. If the number of children — junior age and up — does not exceed 100 to 125, it is reasonable to expect the teacher to handle them in classes of 15 to 25, properly graded and meeting at the church for at least one session weekly of an hour or an hour and a half. Each church will consider its local situation before launching the new program: the public-school schedule, the interest of parents and chil-

dren in church education, the general reaction to the proposal to raise classroom standards to a high level of learning and spiritual growth.

4. Fewer and better classrooms are envisioned, since they can be used several times during the week. In some instances money diverted from enlarging the educational plant — for the purpose of housing everyone at a single session on Sunday mornings — can be used to employ additional pastor-teachers. At any rate, it is desirable for a church to have a woman minister-teacher — preferably the holder of a B.D. degree, but not necessarily ordained — competent to work with preschool and primary children and their parents.

5. Perhaps there should be a trained minister for every fifty to a hundred families in the church, for in addition to thorough teaching of the young there is need for deep and continuing relations between the minister-teacher and the families of children in his or her classes. By providing a pastoral collegium, the large church may shift the present emphasis from program promotion by various specialists to familylike closeness for each group of families as it is served by its particular pastor and finds its identity within the larger Christian fellowship.

6. Many congregations looking toward the sort of teaching and pastoral care entailed in these proposals will need additional professional personnel — hence, more money. Families paying tuition of fifty dollars to seventy-five dollars a year each could finance the undertaking. Given a generation in which to work, the quality of church life and Christian living in society may be expected to show the fruitfulness of this venture. And surely those who are committed to the life of faith within Christian community want the church at the center of their children's concerns

as well as at the center of their own concerns. If this is true, it follows that a radical shift ought to be made from school and community monopoly of youth's time to a reasonable balance between school and community, on the one hand, and the church and Christian allegiances on the other. For how can Christians be content with youth's preoccupation with extracurricular affairs to the neglect of knowledge of their destiny and the worship of God, or with adult's absorption in money and things to the exclusion of love of neighbor and devotion to the God and Father of humankind?

7. Leaders unready to initiate a full program of church education may well begin on a modified basis by following the custom of those pastors presently engaged in teaching a yearlong class in church membership. Eighth- or ninth-grade youth, whether preparing to enter the church or already members, can be taught by their pastor somewhat after the fashion of the late L. A. Convis, as recounted in his book *Adventuring Into the Church.*[3] The next year the teacher might advance with the same pupils into other subject matter, thus gradually adding to his teaching responsibility, for he would also be teaching the incoming membership class. Thereafter he could add a class a year until he is carrying a maximum of six to eight teaching hours, if he is the only pastor of the church; or a larger teaching load, if he is in a church with a multiple ministry and does not do the preaching.

◈

The basic proposition to be elaborated in these pages is that teaching in the church belongs on a par with preaching. The corollary is the need of children and youth no less than adults for a pastor. And by means of guiding the growth of the young in grace and in knowledge, the pastor reaches them and their families at an intimate level for nurture and pastoral care. This may be accomplished both in the small and in the large church, provided the latter establishes a collegium of minister-teachers.

If the Sunday school, as a division of the church, sufficed in the past to bring up children in the life of faith, now the church in its wholeness — with fully qualified professionals doing the teaching — needs to essay the nurture task. Not the traditional Sunday school but church education is requisite for our times, for the day of Biblical knowledge is far spent and the night of Christian faith and hope and love lowers on atomic clouds. Aside from shallow moralisms, too often typical of casual or even pious Sunday school efforts, the profound meaning of Christian belief ought to be articulated and learned. The moment a pastor and his people grasp the importance of nurture and perceive the wisdom of conserving the pastor's time and talent for primary things, that moment a new departure will be taken in Christian teaching and pastoral care. Then will the church as fellowship control the church as institution, and the chosen leader can drop the role of promoter in chief and resume his calling as true shepherd.

As important as anything else in this book is the necessity for all church members to understand just what a valid role for the pastor is. This will concern us at numbers of points, but let it be asserted at once that his is the complex and delicate task of harmonizing within himself the attributes of shepherd and professional leader. As shepherd, his voice and untiring care are to be known by the least of the members of the flock. As professional leader, he is head of other leaders in the church, yet one whose competence does not deteriorate into mere professionalism. Thus he both serves his people in a personal and instructive manner and sees to it that the affairs of his branch of the church of Christ are administered responsibly and efficiently, the while avoiding any taint of exclusiveness associated with an ecclesiastical hierarchy. This being the case, we need not shy away from the idea that his is the main responsibility for classroom teaching; and we may quite properly refer to him as a professional: a pastor, preacher, and teacher. Nonetheless, this servant among servants in the household of God is not to be weighted with an impossible task. Therefore, as we examine the form that his ministry should take, we must see quite clearly just what laymen may do to ensure Christian learning and living.

2

The Church as Educator

READERS wishing to turn immediately to the discussion of establishing a new program of education in the churches may omit this and the next chapter. However, laymen as well as clergymen and seminarians will find these pages germane to the argument.

When Chapters 4 and 5 of this book appeared in the *Andover Newton Bulletin,* in substantially the same form as offered here, one of my superior students censured me for neglecting to discuss the church. (This chapter was already in the hands of the editors of *Religion in Life* and has since been published in the June, 1960, issue.) The student is right, of course; the nature of the church should be reviewed prior to formulating any plan for its educational ministry. And so, faithful to academic procedure, let us engage in a bit of spadework and relate the meaning of the church to education.

What term best denotes the kind of educational endeavor needed in Protestant churches? Increasing concern to articulate theological foundations for education and a desire to be specific about our task have combined to cause dissatisfaction with the term " religious education " as applied to teaching-learning programs in the churches. The terms " Christian education " and " Christian religious education" are often used, but church-related colleges still carry on Christian education, and to speak of Christian religious education is somewhat awkward and redundant. "Christian nurture," despite rich connotations, has had at least a century to catch the fancy of term makers and users of terms, yet it has hardly done so — possibly because the word "nurture" conveys little meaning to the public mind, or perhaps because Horace Bushnell's theology has never been generally accepted. And of course others besides Protestants address themselves to Christian education, to Christian nurture.

What have we left that is clearly ours? Two writers in the field — H. Shelton Smith and Harry C. Munro — speak of Protestant nurture. This is precise. This is what we are engaged in: Protestant nurture, yet this too presents difficulties. Students of this discipline and workers in the field have been willing to be called educators, or religious educators, or Christian educators, but who wants to be known as a Protestant nurturer? Directors of religious education, ministers of Christian education, plain educational directors, yes — though it has been far from easy over the years to be explicit about these titles. I have chosen to use "church education" to designate both the discipline and the task that engage teachers of the Protestant Church. And though this term too is not entirely satisfactory, it has some advantages. As a variation of what was said in Chapter 1, church education may be defined as a teaching-learning enterprise, grounded in theology and Scripture, whose goal is that of enabling persons to learn of God through Christ as experienced in Christian community, the church.

Prof. Paul H. Vieth says that the purposes of the church and its education are the same.[4] Agreed. And a notable study of theological education expresses the purpose of the church as that of increasing the love of God and neighbor.[5] Prof. Howard Grimes, following the late Prof. Lewis J. Sherrill, places nurture within the context of the church redemptive. And so do others, particularly Randolph Crump Miller and his disciples, believing as they do that education for Christian living derives from life within the church, a faith-grace relationship. How shall we view the church?

Paul's conception of it as the body of Christ is fruitful for our thinking, provided we don't become disconcerted by trying to equate a particular church with this imagery. Being members one of another, gathered and knit together by faith in Christ — confident that he discloses the God who loves us — we are organically related, sustained by this knitting and joining as members of a whole greater than our individual selves or even the sum of all the individuals composing it. Our creation is such that there is no meaning, no growth, no sustenance apart from some sort of union, some continuing relationship that overcomes isolation and provides fulfillment for the individual.

But there are drawbacks to this image of the church. Though we speak of the mystical body of Christ, the word "body" almost inevitably is taken too literally, with a physiological connotation. And likening persons unto the parts of a body diminishes them.

A person is always an integer, something of a whole, with a certain autonomy, possessing freedom to approach other persons, and freedom to withdraw, either commingling with them in communion or in part insulating himself from other selves. One *chooses* to commingle, *decides* to relate himself to other people, is free to do so, and free not to do so. We are not forced to be subject to our brothers; never are we compelled against our wills to enter the larger freedom of being members one of another. To be human, to be created in God's image, is to have the final say as to whether or not we shall enter into fellowship one with another and with God. Nevertheless, we deny our creation and stunt our growth if we elect to be a stranger, separated from others and alienated from God. We need community as earth needs its atmosphere. And for overcoming alienation from our fellows and God, both community and communion are essential. Created for community with our fellows, we are fashioned in the image of God and dependent upon communion with him as he, in the Holy Spirit, dwells in his church.

It may be said categorically that the life of the church — the quality of living and worshiping and acting and thinking of a particular church — educates individuals and the fellowship as a whole. This education is a process of growth in Christ, available for all ages and carried on informally as well as formally, incidentally as well as intentionally, unconsciously as well as deliberately. The church is requisite for growth in grace and knowledge of our Lord, for anyone — young or old — and for all groups, children's classes no less than adults' societies. In the informed and purposive church, persons are understood and materials of instruction are selected with the clear intent to bring about individual and corporate experiences with God. Experience is the key word here, and the dominant desire of the church is to create relationships wherein the God of Christ is met, apprehended, worshiped.

The church that advances its mission as educator is dedicated to expending intelligent effort in helping its children, youth, and adults to love God with their minds, and hearts, and with all the given and learned powers of their whole being, powers of perception and devotion. The church as educator does not leave to God the whole job of nurturing people. Helping people to grow Godward is a human responsibility, a vocation, mutually undertaken by all gathered in the church. As educator, the church knows that God acts first, in love seeking and inviting his creatures to enter into redemptive relations with him. But more than simple human response to divine action is involved; creative interaction marks redemptive relationship — not dull reaction on our part, but profound experience in which God and we, his creatures, commune together. On the human level, this communion means relationship, the nature of which is quite other than one's acting and another's merely responding.

So, also, with relationship on the divine-human level. I am persuaded to believe that a theological position that leaves all the initiative up to God belittles his creatures. We humans can do more than respond, though assuredly we may do no less. Indeed, if God really has fashioned us, he has endowed us with initiative, nor can I suppose that he expects us to express initiative in every life situation except with respect to him. Rather, I believe he endows us with initiative to be used and invites us to engage in creative communion with him by means of interrelationship.

This is not to say that relationship with God permits human willfulness or presumption. Humans dare not attempt to impinge on the Almighty. What I do wish to say emphatically is that creative communion between God and those who would know him — loving him with their whole mind — is the occasion not only for worship and enjoyment but also for critical inquiry. It is a kind of testing of the validity of God's truth in so far as human intelligence and experience permit. So it is that one who either questions in order that he may know, or voices sincere religious doubt, is to be regarded as being on the threshold of what may become his own very personal, very meaningful experience with God, provided only that churchmen — lay and cleric — have the grace to show the seeker and the doubter that persons in Christ are knit and joined together in true relationship.

True relationship means love of God and neighbor. The nurture process develops this love by means of growth in grace and knowledge guided by the church. From an educational perspective growth is always sought as the one indispensable of aim and process. From the Biblical perspective this growth in knowledge denotes personal communion with Christ. A doctrine of the church may well argue that not knowledge about Christ so much as experience with him is sought. To experience God is to worship him, and the church is a worshiping community. It is also a community of inquiry, an environment productive of human and divine interaction.

This word " interaction " requires explication. In this context it may be defined as contact of personality with personalities, involvement of persons with each other and the Person of Christ, during which there is a flow of concern — power and spirit and meaning — between God and his creatures. Does he not still rejoice with us, on occasion grieve over us, and strive with us as with his Galilean companions?

If you shrink from this line of thought, fearing that it leads to a demeaning of the Absolute, of him who is perfect, I reply that the God who opens himself to communing with us remains the Absolute, the same yesterday and today; he never takes on our relative natures. But he is the God of Christ, this same Jesus Christ who was tempted like ourselves, but who, unlike us, yields not to temptation. And our God is nearer than hands and feet, never afar off, for he enters into relationship with us. Of course he is other than man, yet if we had the wisdom of the child, we would know that he is with us, among us, acting upon us, acting *with* us — in so far as we accept his grace (what Prof. Daniel Williams calls the whole of his love in action) — sometimes acting against us, whenever we will to thwart his will that in him we may be made whole.

And we are acting upon him, our powers sometimes resisting him, sometimes neutral toward him, sometimes uniting with his power. Because our God is sensitive, is he not by nature responsive to us? And if he is responsive, he is affected by us, affected not to deviate one iota from his changelessness, but to open himself, so to speak, ever wider to us in our pitiable and tragic needs. Perhaps it is not too much to speak of Infinite Love as ever expanding, precisely because the church — the body of Christ — proves so imperfect.

We humans, gathered in the church, knit together in the body of Christ, meet God, learn of him, and affect him. In a sense we contribute to release of a greater abundance of grace given to make us more ready to stand before our Father, God, whose judgment of his church is absolute righteousness, whose justice is love, whose love embraces the church in creative interaction. I have said we contribute to release of God's grace; we do not *cause* it, perhaps we do not evoke it — for it is always there, a free gift — but we do *invoke* it. This we do when we are interacting creatively within the church — within the body whose head is Christ, within the community animated by the Holy Spirit wherein God continues to reveal himself to us.

God the Father comes to prophet and saint in their solitude; Christ is present in his body, the church; and the Holy Spirit meets the gathered company of human individuals in which his nurturing power is released. And until the gathered company actually experiences the enabling power of God's grace made manifest in the Holy Spirit, a church is less than the church; it is a collection of individuals. Just as the kinship family remains but a number of individuals save as individualism is qualified by the mind and mood of the family unit, so the church fails to break through its institutionalized form except it become itself, a communion of saints wherein the individual is subject unto the brethren because they are caught up in the Lord. Again, even as a class is only an aggregation of individuals save as interaction, mutuality, and organic relations prevail, so is a church only an organization of disparate selves unless those selves become unified in love for one another and God.

Hence we conclude that prior to a church's being ready to nurture a novice in grace and knowledge of God, it must really be the church, the household of God in which people are no more strangers and foreigners but fellow citizens with the saints (Eph. 2:19). As theologically unrespectable as The Letter of James may be today in some circles, I take it that there is wisdom here; yea more, there is truth. For example: " Draw near to God and he will draw near to you." (James 4:8.) The church as educator ought always to strive to lead its communicants into God's presence, and by any test of experience and insight I submit that entering into his presence will be seen as taking place in the measure that persons come to God through the fellowship, the church. Created for community, our complete growth is only afforded by means of Christian community.

In true community people hold all things in common: their creaturehood, their aspirations to be creative, their resources and interests. In fellowship persons regard each other with concern. Both the joy and the sorrow of anyone are joy and sorrow of all. Rest and labor, triumph and defeat, grace and sin, love and enmity in one affect all. In other words, the life of each is the life of the fellowship, when the fellows are united in Christ. The household of God is the family of God, and if we are in Christ, we are new creatures, by his grace enabled to transcend our partial selves and restore the defaced fellowship that marks the church that fails to be Christian community.

How does this community come into being? And by what miracle can any given church that you may now have in mind truly rise above pettiness, pride, complacency, foolishness, enmity, and strife? Perhaps it is not very helpful to reply that a church becomes a Christian fellowship when God's gift of himself, in grace and love, is accepted. Nor are we satisfied by the reminder that his gift of his church will be appropriated by us only as we elect to receive it. Rather, let us understand that we are called upon to expend worshipful and intelligent effort to bring the fellowship into fullness of being.

Paul reminds us that he plants, Apollos waters, and God gives the increase. Nevertheless, planting and sustaining are inseparable from growth; and the work of God in creating and ultimately bringing the Christian fellowship to fruition is accomplished in and through us. It is not that God neatly divides his task from ours and tells us, " Do this bit, then stand aside and I'll carry on." It is, rather, that we are to know ourselves joined with him in the process of actualizing the fellowship that is ours provisionally. God provides it; with him we must bring it into full being. Verily, a church that is a church, a fellowship that is in

Christ, is not handed to us or thrust upon us by the Father of our Lord Jesus Christ. Ours is the responsibility for learning to live in fellowship. This learning entails a life-long educational process.

Just as a child's growth in the family ought to be preceded by rich learning on the part of the parents — the better for them and their children to grow along together — so older people in Christian fellowship are to grow in grace and knowledge as a sure means for readying the fellowship to assume its Christian vocation of nurturing babes in the Lord. It is out of the overflow of adult development that children are nourished in their initial stages. And later, as years and experience mount, it is out of the continuing relationship between young and old in Christian fellowship that individuals attain maturity in Christ.

Recall the educational principle that learning is living and living is learning. Although we do not necessarily learn by experience — witness the world's repeated resorting to war despite its futility for settling differences — it is only in and through experience that we can learn. To learn is to change. Considered change in conduct and value makes the difference between realization of one's gifts and powers and deterioration of the person and society. Adults can learn, do learn, thereby enlarging their worth not alone to themselves but to the human community.

Learning-theory and the grace of God must be considered together, at least when the problem of spiritual motivation is considered. A venerated teacher and colleague of other years denied this, maintaining that not grace but simple human decision motivates any kind of learning. But consider the most difficult of all learning tasks — that of learning to love an unlovable person. This, I think, is not accomplished simply by deciding to love him. Granted that one's decision may start the act of learning, and that a severely disciplined will gets the process well under way, I rather doubt that you and I, in and of ourselves, are able to complete this learning, for it involves such a thoroughgoing change in us, such an unreasonable and unnatural intent, that ordinarily we are powerless to carry it through. It is just here, I think, that the grace of God so empowers us that we are able to love the hitherto unlovable one. In one sense, grace is the motivation; in another sense, motivation — the power to see the learning task through to a conclusion — is a combination of one's own decision and the grace of God. Thus a task impossible for you or me, acting alone, becomes possible by God's acting in us. His gracious dispensation empowers us to learn to love, to be reconciled with persons toward whom we feel enmity.

Or take another illustration. Here is a person who elects to exercise forbearance and kindness despite his proneness to quick irritation or harsh judgment. Business, home, and church relationships leave him enervated, if not depleted, and threaten to pull him over the brink into contentiousness; yet if he is renewed by grace, so that characteristically he practices forbearance and kindness, and the other fruits of the Spirit, he is growing into maturity in Christ. That this sort of growth occurs is testified to over and over even by people who by temperament and habit are inclined to produce far more fruits of evil than fruits of righteousness.

Another educational principle holds that we learn that which we practice with satisfaction. Certainly the experience of grace affords the ultimate satisfaction, and to taste the achievement of having learned to be patient and kind and joyful and forgiving and loving, realizing that we are growing, is most rewarding.

A distinctly Christian principle of learning, then, is this:

nurture in the faith depends on growth in grace, and the church is requisite for this growth. Now, as in New Testament times, Christians are to strive for growth in grace and knowledge of the Lord (II Peter 3:18). If we learn our lesson of grace, we live it not only in the church but also in the world; for example, in interracial relations.

Currently it is the United States Supreme Court that prompts a good deal of the tortuous advance toward interracial justice in America. But the Court is unequal to teaching people to love those on the other side of the color line; it cannot re-educate attitudes and refashion habits. Through the centuries we have heard with the hearing of the ear that in Christ there is neither Jew nor Greek, neither bond nor free, but only now, for us — in this land, in these fateful days — is this truth beginning to reach from the brain to the viscera, from the nervous system to facial and vocal muscles, from the mind to the act of physical association, so that we join with Negroes and other minorities among us and attain unto genuine oneness in Christ. The frank admission sometimes heard is entirely true: " In my mind I know all men are my brothers, but I can't *feel* it's so." That, I pause to add, is an example of incomplete learning because God's grace has not taken over. Being incomplete, it leaves a vast realm in which the Christian may strive for growth. But spiritual growth will not come about by simply relying on personal or corporate merit. All aspiring, all our intentions to be brotherly, all individual and collective goodness, lack a dimension of love essential for learning brotherliness. How different the story when we recognize our limitations and turn to the grace of God, given in love to enable us to be loving!

Who among us can doubt that the church's most central task in this hour is that of fostering growth in grace? There are practical ways to proceed. Let me mention a few.

Presently the uneasy conscience of an appreciable number of Christians makes them ready to probe more deeply the meaning and imperative of the gospel. A variety of fresh approaches to church education ought to be made in a spirit of " Come, let us reason together," and " Lord, what would you have me do? " Prof. John L. Casteel's *Spiritual Renewal Through Personal Groups* records the ventures of various adult groups in learning to live the gospel. In numbers of churches around the country, formal adult classes are being supplemented by study groups arising more or less spontaneously in quest of fuller understanding of the Bible and the meaning of Christian faith. One such group read and discussed among themselves Paul S. Minear's *Eyes of Faith* and D. M. Baillie's *God Was in Christ.* Only now and then was the minister's aid requested by these laymen whose spiritual hunger, interest, and intelligence motivated their explorations. Some informal church groups continue year after year, alternating Biblical and doctrinal study with attention to child development and the nature of the Christian family, and not forgetting to enjoy recreation together; thereby personal friendship is deepened while men and women quicken the life of the churches.

Nor should we overlook the possibilities contained in existing organizations in the church — for instance, in official boards — for growth in Christian grace. There are churches enlivened and enriched by boards that educate themselves by continuing study, thereby deepening personal and corporate faith. Instead of being enmeshed in routine functions, these organizations handle their business with dispatch and then address themselves to such issues as stewardship and the world mission of the church, thus subjecting the activities of the local church to the test of the Christian imperative.

An example of a denomination's approach to adult nurture is the Parish Life Conference used by the Episcopal Church. At its best the Conference weaves the principles and procedures of social psychology into the practice of Christian fellowship and demonstrates ways by which local churches may learn to be the church, a redeeming and nurturing community essential for both adult and child growth.

And who can miss the educative and redemptive power imbuing persons when a major social and spiritual problem is met and handled lovingly and sacrificially, as in Montgomery under the leadership of Martin Luther King? [6] One may say that to the extent that churches welcome present opportunities to resolve racial and other staggering problems in a spirit of brotherliness, they are realizing their maximum growth in Christ. This is how we learn to live by the grace of God. The Christian community, the church as educator, is the medium by which its communicants discover that they can learn Christian truth as they live it.

Foundational to our educational work is theology, an expression of what experience with God means to the Christian community. It is the church that nurtures persons in grace and knowledge of Christ, thus increasing love of God and neighbor. When adult nurture is vital the fellowship is providing an atmosphere conducive to productive nurture of children. Dissatisfaction with the nature and accomplishments of religious education suggests the need for a more incisive education wherein learners at all ages enter into a continuing experience with God. This experience may be known simply as church education.

3

The Meaning of Church Education

WITHIN a few years after its organization in 1922, the International Council of Religious Education, influenced by men like Prof. William C. Bower, of the University of Chicago, and Prof. George A. Coe, long of Columbia University and Union Seminary, began to show the effect of empiricism and its reliance on the scientific method of general education. About a decade later religious education was fighting to preserve its experimentalism against the claims of neo-orthodoxy.[7] And with the publication of Lewis J. Sherrill's final book in 1955, *The Gift of Power*, experimentalism was replaced with revelation as the core of Christian nurture.

The import of Sherrill's writing and teaching is that educational work in the churches needs refashioning both with respect to curriculum and procedures, for the task before us belongs to the church as the redemptive community. For him the nurture process is inherent in the nature of the church, the people of God in relation to the Person of Jesus Christ. This emphasis has prompted the curriculum committee of the Division of Christian Education of the National Council of Churches to rethink the gospel message and search for educational principles and procedures more consistent with the purposes of the church than with general or religious education. Significantly, since 1950, education of co-operating churches has been organized under the National Council of Churches instead of the displaced International Council of Religious Education. Not religious education, therefore, but church education concerns us, and we need a new statement of principles to guide the nurture process in the churches.

Let us juxtapose religious education and church education, the better to understand their differences.

First, religious education assumes the possibility of finding truth within the present experience of learners as they draw upon the heritage of the church, a record of past experiences. Church education more fully accepts the Bible and its gospel message as the norm of faith and life. However, being Protestant, church education is not authoritarian but authoritative.

There is a vast difference between setting out, on the one hand, to discover what may be an unknown or only sensed truth, and on the other, starting with a faith that has stood the test of centuries and therefore claims to be true. In the one instance, exploration and experimentation are primary; in the other, assimilation and dogma. The former appeals mainly to firsthand experience; the latter seems to stress remote or vicarious experience. The one is pragmatic and tentative; the other, transmissive and definite. Central in religious education is quest; central in church education is response to what has already been found. Moreover, religious education encourages nonconformity to authority while church education appears to require conformity. Hence it is easy to see why religious education fears indoctrination and transmission of the heritage and addresses itself rather to reconstruction of religion and the human order. But church education, rightly understood, goes beyond mere transmission of the Christian heritage and refuses to be hobbled by dogmas, for its chief aim is to guide persons in the power of the Holy Spirit into relations with their fellows and the Person of Jesus Christ. Accordingly, it is no less dynamic than religious education.

Although religious education is convinced that truth is best learned experimentally, in its Protestant expression it has also taken as its goal growth in Christlikeness. Furthermore, for the most part, modern religious education has consistently sought to bring the religious tradition to bear upon the learner's present experience. But the feeling will not down that its leaders have been too closely allied with the pragmatists of general education.

During the first thirty-five or forty years of this century George A. Coe was to religious education what John Dewey was to general education, and each movement had its effect on the other. Coe acknowledged his indebtedness to Dewey, but he made his own contribution to the development of progressive general education (as James D. Smart, Harry C. Munro, and others have recognized). Because Coe was thoroughly committed to the educational process, he adopted much of its genius and in so doing influenced other leaders in the field, notably Harrison S. Elliott and William C. Bower, men committed to an empirical rather than a dogmatic approach to religious education. Hence it is not hard to perceive why religious education has been so readily associated with Dewey and his idea that "there is nothing to which education is subordinate save more education." "The educational process has no end beyond itself; it is its own end." [8]

We cannot, of course, let these statements of Dewey stand out of context. Actually he made education the servant of the child and American democracy. His experimentalism assumed a value system — a faith, if you please — within which it operated; and it had aims, ends in view other than simply more education. Likewise, experimental religious education has intended to serve growing persons, in its Protestant form guiding them into Christlike living and toward a reconstruction of life.[9] In truth, though using the experimental method, religious education has not imitated Dewey's pragmatism but has sought to lead persons to God through Christian living. Vaguely theological, it has professed to be thoroughly educational. Indeed it mistrusts traditional theology, while failing to work out a clear theology in which to ground itself.

Let us underscore this observation: The religious educator has always been willing to rely on the educational process to bring people to truth; and he is confident that nurture is more effective than proclamation or transmission of dogma. For him doctrine is not the point at which the educational process is initiated. Learners are to begin not where those who have already learned leave off but at the point of their own experience and concern. For some religious educators neither a doctrine of revelation nor any other is conceived of as having very much relevance for Christian nurture. The heritage is considered subordinate if not inconsequential to present experience, and the need of learners to engage in meaningful activities productive of the good life. And the good life is to be nurtured according to the insights of liberal theology, principles of child development, educational psychology, sociology, and cultural anthropology.

Church education also uses the sciences of man, and much that is emphasized by religious education is quite acceptable as an aid in Christian growth. But church educators fear that revealed truth — that which is recorded in the Bible and by faith accepted within the historic and contemporary Christian community — is neglected by the experimentalists; and this despite their intention to guide growing persons into Christlike living. Aside from being a source book tapped by religious educators to further the growth of learners, the Bible for church educators is a record of God's disclosure of himself and his dealings with his creation. Scripture testifies to the truth about God and humankind and is given in order that persons may know salvation. The church educator grants that this viewpoint opens the door wide for overemphasis on content and for teaching as mere instruction, but he believes these dangers can be avoided and that full consideration can be given to individual and corporate need to experience God in the Person of Christ. Most assuredly the Word of God made flesh — the Christ — rather than simply the words of God in the Book, is both the point of departure and the continuing concern of church education. So it is that while giving more attention to Biblical content and church doctrine than religious education does, church education is not content-centered but Person-centered. The implications in this statement will be spelled out in our final chapter.

Secondly, religious education, something of an alien movement within the churches, has tended to work more or less independently of them, as a sort of parallel enterprise. Church education is the church expressing itself in the nurturing process.

Modern religious education roots back in the thinking of Horace Bushnell, the New England clergyman who, at the middle of the nineteenth century, broke with the theology of his day and its insistence that the child remains in sin until he undergoes a conversion experience. Granting that some become Christian through conversion, Bushnell pressed the point that there are Biblical grounds for believing that nurture is the normative way to salvation and — in words oft-quoted — asserted that " a child is to grow up a Christian and never know himself otherwise." [10]

Toward the turn of the century the impact of Biblical criticism was felt in this country and liberal theology was spreading. Meantime, educational psychology and experimental schools were calling attention to the child, his nature and needs. Educators and religionists came together in 1903 and founded the Religious Education Association, an interfaith body that reflected not only the above developments but also the optimistic mood of the times. Prior to the First World War social progress and human brotherhood seemed ascendant, and many there were who believed that the Kingdom of God was assured by evolutionary stages. The idea of human perfectability was certainly not universal, but it carried pronounced weight with humanitarians and religionists alike. It seems fair to say that implicit in the religious education movement was the tenet that salvation of the individual and society derives from the educational process instead of the New Testament and Reformation doctrine of justification by faith.

From its beginning until recently, modern religious education has stressed human resourcefulness to the neglect of attending to God's action. And perhaps the life of faith — at the adult level — leaned too heavily upon sense data and reason, and — at the child's level — upon learning and growth as a consequence of guided activities.

Church education propounds the doctrine that nurture in Christ begins when the faith of the church is communicated by love to the child who is capable of trust. This education develops the learner's faith and, under the direction of the Christian community, moves on to include reason. For the young child the first ingredient of faith is trust; trust in persons who love him, whom he sees; trust that in later years becomes his love of God whom he and no one can see — except with the eyes of faith focused on Jesus Christ. The child at any age, the adolescent, the adult all through life, continues to need a structure of faithful human relationships to sustain his faith, establish his belief, enlighten his thinking. This is the mission of the church as the continuing revelation of God, for as God is in Christ so is the Holy Spirit in the church. By faith we know this; by reason — reflective thinking in the church class, study group, and elsewhere — we reinforce what we know, remembering that it is not reason that embraces faith but faith that embraces reason.

Now if religious education seeks to draw growing persons into the educative process in order to effect Christlike changes in them, church education purposes to help the church *be* the church and work its work of grace within the community experiencing Christ and nurturing persons through trust in human relations, the better to ensure the fruition of love of God and a world of neighbors.

Thirdly, religious education has given itself to character development through the enriching of experience, reevaluation of values, scientific thinking, problem-solving. Church education probes the depths of personality and strives to effect reconciliation between person and person, between person and God.

Since the Character Education inquiry, conducted by Hugh Hartshorne and associates in the 1920's, religious educators have recognized that character is achieved as a by-product of effective social functioning. William C.

Bower and others, like the majority of the spokesmen for general education, have held that character develops through creative experience. And so it does. We can be thankful for the contributions these men have made toward our understanding of how persons may grow toward Christlikeness.

The church educator is not disposed to call religious education to account for failure to go deeply enough into human personality, understanding its pitiable deficiency, its tragic condition. Rather, he desires to give a different emphasis to personality and character development, not bypassing the growth process but using it to go beyond where social theorists have generally left off, advancing to the very point at which serious account is taken of man's sinfulness: his alienation from himself, from his fellows, and from God. Like the psychiatrist, the church educator knows that the human individual — the child, the adolescent, the adult — is a divided soul, in need of atoneness with himself, in need of healthy relations with his kind. And like the Biblical theologian, the church educator perceives that reconciliation with God is fundamental to gaining atoneness with self and others.

Can there be any doubt today that the human condition is one of acute anxiety? It is ironic that our generation has been so concerned to avoid engendering fears in children that we have left them in the worse plight of anxiety, an anxiety that is perhaps as intense and poignant as that of adults. And we have compounded irony by reiterating God's love, soft-pedaling his judgment and wrath, only to widen the separation of both adults and children from God.

In my boyhood it was the fad for young people to hurl at each other the epithet " You sinner! " Whether merely a slang expression or evidence of theological prescience, I know not, but I rather think it was along about then that I began wondering if a child belongs in the category of certain mysterious adults labeled sinners. Later on I accepted the view that children are not sinful but are subject to error and immaturity. I reasoned that until the age of accountability, surely the God of righteousness refuses to bracket the child with the adult sinner — the child who by nature thrives on affection and is quick to forgive.

And yet it must be said that at every stage of its existence the emerging personality is involved in sin, as truly as it is in love. Sin is a part of the human condition wherein an individual's willfulness damages interpersonal relations. A quality of destructiveness inheres in the will and the young child has the power to hurt; for example, by prolongation of what Prof. Ross Snyder (in another connection) calls " mean feelings." True, the child does not comprehend the significance of his attitudes and actions, but early in life (and just how early no one can say) it is probable that he has some apprehension of what he is doing when he makes his parents and others around him suffer. And this he sometimes does when the fault is clearly his and not his parents', resisting love as fully as an adolescent does when he scorns what he knows to be justice meted out to him in love.

Let us be very clear about this issue. Early childhood negativism, even prolonged and precocious hostility, is not to be equated with rebellion against God. A child yet too young to be a self — although already " a candidate for personality " (Bushnell's phrase) — is as incapable of defying God as he was in the prenatal stage. Nor is a tantrum blasphemy, though it does represent the dross of human relations, dross perhaps necessary for giving a certain

strength to the developing person and durability to the
gold of interpersonal relations. It may be added that however patient and just and loving the parent is, he has to be
resisted in some measure if the child is to become a self,
achieve integrity. It follows that to be human is, in some
degree, to be involved in the feeling and practice of
alienation.

But all this sounds as if I think there are only children
of darkness in this world. There are also children of light.
More accurately, each child is a child of light *and* darkness, born with possibilities for good and evil. Created in
the image of God, often nurtured by parents whose love is
of God himself, nevertheless, the child is early infected
with sin, be he ever so attracted to goodness, be he ever so
consistently loved. He, as definitely as an adolescent,
knows he stands in need of forgiveness, therefore when he
is developmentally capable of altruism — normally around
the age of nine — we ought to teach him that he, like us
his seniors, is a sinner, yet loved by God who is always
ready to reclaim him.

A word of caution is needed here. Church educators
must remember that whatever the child's responsibility
for marring the image of God in which he is born, he in-
herits the common lot of humankind, which is rebellion
against, as well as an affinity for, goodness. This is the human dilemma. In his fumbling effort to appropriate and
express the freedom potentially his by virtue of his creation, the child experiences estrangement at an emotional
level before he can conceptualize it. He lives with it during the years in which conscience is developing, about the
ages three to eight or nine when normally he is establishing the ego and outgrowing self-centeredness. And I suspect that even earlier he senses the conflict between his

growth need to be over against the adults who minister to him and his desire to reciprocate their affection for him. Call this conflict the pain of growth, if you will, it remains evidence that the human condition is fraught with alienation.

Nor is this all. The child's plight is worsened because he is too immature to distinguish between justifiable and unjustifiable resistance to adult authority. He is likely to resist not only the wrong and evil but also the right and good in the parent, and though his initial motive for resisting is largely the necessary one of unconscious striving to establish the self, the faulty and immature way by which he proceeds reinforces his alienation and sometimes delays the growth of the self he is seeking, and may eventuate in secondary motives that cause him in late childhood to delight in evil. Thus even before he is fully a self, such a child is marred by the wrong kind of separateness — for there is a separateness that produces essential and justifiable individuality while respecting other individuals — and the possibility of his future at-onement with God is diminished. This is sickness of such seriousness as to preclude development of the self and conscience. So far as a given child is concerned one can only say that he may or may not be more sinned against than sinner; his condition, which began partly because of inadequate interpersonal relations, may or may not end in chronic sin. For the amoral personality, for the psychopath, there is the diagnosis " illness "; for the " normal," the " responsible " child, we are left with the designation " sinner."

Fourthly, religious education concentrates on the good life in this world. Church education envisions life in time and eternity.

It is instructive to note that religious education, social

ethics, and liberal theology flourished at about the same time in the seminaries, three decades or so ago. Each of these disciplines drew heavily upon the social gospel. It could be argued that the religious education movement, spearheaded by Coe, went farther in addressing itself to the problem of creating the good life — the Kingdom of God in time — than general education has gone toward changing the social order. Early in its history the International Council of Religious Education included among the objectives of Christian education one that would " develop in growing persons the ability and disposition to participate in and contribute constructively to the building of a social order throughout the world, embodying the ideal of the Fatherhood of God and the brotherhood of man." [11]

Unhappily the course of history has forced the idealistic and optimistic outlook of the recent past to fade. Today we live with the dark knowledge that there is so little time, that there is no place to hide. The physicist's second law of thermodynamics, postulating the eventual end of life on this planet caused by gradual cooling of the sun, has been superseded by the stark prospect of global incineration by release of atomic and hydrogen heat. Modern man may be about to awaken to the likelihood that all his aspirations and works are meaningless save as he sees possibility of life with God beyond earth and time, in heaven and eternity. The Biblical faith thus becomes abruptly relevant, and death is at last perceived as but an episode in time.

Make no mistake about it: currently children do wonder, do fear, are gripped by anxiety greater than adults imagine. Both for children and for thoughtful adults, any teaching about the protection of a loving, all-powerful God only mocks reality unless it embraces the Biblical faith that creatures of this earth all along have been destined to become inhabitants of God's eternal realm, there to live with him. Therefore, nurture within the church — within the household of God and in its branches, kinship families — is under the imperative to be forthright at each moment of wondering, hoping, doubting, fearing, when child or adult wants to be told the truth about his destiny. This truth simply cannot be conveyed within an educational framework or process preoccupied with life on earth. It must testify to the Biblical hope of life in God's transcendent realm.

How depict this realm? Here the supreme act of faith is to be shared with the child by the adult of mature faith, mature confidence, quietly, simply, admitting to limited knowledge, yet testifying to the profound joy known to the soul whose hope is fixed on God. It was ever thus in facing the prospect of personal death — and every child ponders death; it is acutely relevant at this moment in human history.

So it is that church educators must deal with Christian hope no less than with Christian faith. Perhaps we understand how to nurture the life of faith better than we do the life of hope. And, like child-development spokesmen and psychiatrists, educators have provided more insight into the process of learning to love than has been provided for helping persons to grow up in faith and hope. We must teach and live as if the fate of the world depends on us as individuals, as citizens of the world, even as we confess that human destiny is ultimately in the hands of God.

Now the purpose of religious education to contribute to the building of a brotherhood under God is also the purpose of church education for just as long as life may last. For both time and beyond time concern the church, with respect to its faith and its works. Even now were the church to be the church — the yeast of redemption within the bread of the world — it might bring into being a global community of a merit exceeding the dearest vision of the social gospelers. This possibility lies within Christian hope, and it is out of hope that we both live and teach. The reverse possibility is also to be kept in mind; namely, that men and earth could be obliterated in fantastic warfare. But this in no wise destroys Christian hope; it only increases the need for church education to bring children and youth and adults to terms with the possibility of the world's end. Like the prospect of personal death that of planetary extinction is encompassed by Christian hope, and by the Pauline conviction that whether we die or live is gain for each one who is in the Lord. This is the confident outlook that the church is to foster in its members as they — both children and adults — contemplate time and eternity.

I have contrasted religious education and church education in an attempt to see the direction in which church education purports to move. I have suggested first, that the one assumes the possibility of finding truth, the other looks to the Bible for its norm of faith and life; secondly, religious education has tended to work more or less independently of the church, whereas church education *is* the church expressing itself in the nurture process; thirdly, religious education has given itself to character development; church education probes the depths of personality and strives for reconciliation between the individual and his God; and fourthly, religious education concentrates on the good life in this world; church education envisions life in time and eternity.

It may be hoped that church education, where possible, will build upon modern religious education. The two are not wholly opposite, either in conception or in program; furthermore, religious education has been useful to the Christian church. It now becomes the task of the church to minister according to the fullness and richness of its being, as a worshiping community teaching by influence and by systematic pastoral instruction.

4

A Design for Teaching

IN OUR DAY the impression is strong that products of Protestant Sunday schools know little about the Bible and less about the meaning of Christian faith. One hears of college instructors who lament the fact that students seldom catch a literary allusion to the Bible; and surveys by professors of religion repeatedly demonstrate former Sunday school pupils' almost total lack of knowledge of Old Testament events, and New Testament teaching. And everywhere there are cries of distress because religious knowledge remains elementary. Consequently, at best, literary tastes are cheapened and understanding of the Christian heritage so deficient as to cause many leaders and friends of the Sunday schools to conclude that they are unequal to the teaching task of the church. At worst, youth are deprived of saving knowledge of God in whose church they have been misled by inept teaching.

What do church leaders, parents, and young people really expect to be accomplished within the usual type of educational program in our churches? After more than a century and a half of Sunday school work sponsored by the churches in this country, and despite all the investment of devotion, effort, time, and money, are the results satisfactory to anyone?

Luther and other Reformation leaders perceived that an informed Protestantism requires ability to read and understand the Bible, hence their emphasis on education. Wesley saw great promise in the Sunday schools and supported them enthusiastically. I doubt not that a considerable proportion of the persons in the Reformation and Evangelical tradition are ready to agree that Protestant Christianity must always depend upon an educated and intelligent priesthood of all believers, and that evangelism and education complement each other in the upbuilding of our churches. We realize that the American scene made sectarian teaching inadvisable in publicly supported schools. Quite rightly the propagation of the several doctrines among us was delegated to the various denominations. That is past history, but a history that turned to the Sunday schools ought now to be made to take a new tack.

Visualize, if you will, a boy or girl about to graduate from high school, expecting either to go to college or to enter immediately upon a life career. Remember that general education knows rather precisely what it ought to have achieved up to this point with this youth, both as a person and a student. But does the Sunday school know what it should have accomplished with this same young person? What do you and I want him to have from church education?

◇

First of all, we covet for every young person intelligent commitment to Christ as Lord and Savior. As a person, we desire that the eighteen-year-old shall walk humbly with his God, loving mercy and doing justly. With all his maturing adequacy — his ability to think clearly, to co-operate and contribute to the common good, resisting evil — we expect him to realize that self-sufficiency needs to yield to the all-sufficiency of the God of Christ, the elder brother. The youth nurtured in faith, hope, and love is one who bears within himself the courage and compassion of a disciple of Jesus Christ. He is an advocate of truth who has learned that the greatest among us must be servant of all. The boy or girl nurtured in Christian virtue from childhood to the threshold of adult life is distinguished by an integrity surpassing that of those who have not communed with the anointed of God; such a young person is *expected* to be devoted to Christ, and if he is not — if the fruits of his living show that he is not in fact experiencing God's love — then we must conclude that the fault is not the youth's alone, but also that of the kind of nurture he has had.

After allowing for the limitations of formal teaching, the acquisition of knowledge of right and wrong, and the learning of essential facts of the Christian heritage, we are still left with the need to lean heavily on the nurture process in the work of the church. As we do so, we shall be aware that beyond the hearing of the ear and the appropriating with the mind, we desire that each learner shall know and love Him — above all others — who is the way, the truth, and the life. Commitment to the living Christ is paramount if growing persons are really to know God. Education simply for the acquisition of knowledge — even knowledge about God — is not our ultimate goal. We realize that there are dangers in undue emphasis on an intellectual approach to church education, but nurture remains the most dependable means we humans have to bring our young into a continuing relationship with the Christ who transforms them. Basic in nurture is study, learning, knowledge. And though knowledge isn't necessarily virtue, neither is there any virtue in ignorance.

We aspire, then, to provide solid knowledge, the meat and not merely the milk of the gospel. And providing it, we expect it to be assimilated.

The high school graduate, as the product also of the church's teaching, ought to be able to read the Bible with enjoyment and profit. That this elementary goal is never reached by a good many adults as well as youths is demonstrated by the way they stumble over words and miss the meaning of the Scripture they undertake to read orally. The product of the church's classrooms ought to understand the essential unity of the Bible and know the central message of its books, together with the historic conditions out of which they were written. History, poetry, drama, narrative, doctrine, and exegesis are to be differentiated and understood. Further, highlights in church history — particularly the significance of the Reformation — the rise of the major denominations, the world mission of the church, all lie within the range of understanding and latent interest of the young person capable of graduating from a respectable high school. Moreover, as the aim of general education is effective citizenship, so the aim of church education is participation in Christian community by each youth as worshiper and disciple.

We turn now to a preliminary discussion of how pastoral teaching may function in different church situations. Three types are cited.

1. *Suburban Church* with a membership of fifteen hundred has two ministers and employs six students from a neighboring seminary to assist in the pastoral and teaching program. The annual budget approximates $100,000, of which about $35,000 is allocated to salaries. The church school has an enrollment of 710, including about 200 junior, 150 junior high, and 120 senior high pupils. Most of the

others in the school are young children. The curriculum is planned by the education board under the leadership of a minister assigned to the educational program. At present the teaching is done not only by laymen and seminary students but also by both ministers, each of whom has a section of the ninth grade for a full year during which pupils are prepared for church membership. The ninth-grade classes are held in place of regular church school classes and are integral to the curriculum. One minister meets his section on Sunday morning, the other on a week-day. The work is comprehensive and requires preparation and examinations, with the result that interest remains high throughout the year. Pupils and their parents appreciate the classes.

Now note that these two ministers are teachers. Their classroom standards are respected and the learning that takes place is on a par with that in the excellent public schools afforded by the high socioeconomic status of the community. Note also that one of these sections meets on a weekday, and this in a community crowded with after-school activities and homework for children, and a multiplicity of civic, church, and personal affairs for adults. The weekday class is better attended than regular Sunday school classes, partly because families frequently go off for weekend outings, and partly because the Sunday school — quite understandably — is considered trivial. Given a choice between the ordinary Sunday school class — taught by a layman with less than adequate training in Bible, theology, church history, and principles of education — and a class taught by a minister who knows these fields and children, what child or parent would not prefer the latter?

Presently the ministers are considering scheduling more

classes during the week, and fewer on Sunday, with the hope of maintaining better attendance and improving the quality of the church's teaching. Significantly, Suburban Church has already made a start, whether it knows it or not, in the direction in which it ought to move; that is, toward arranging weekday classes taught by the ministers for all pupils, at least those from junior age through high school.

In round numbers these five hundred pupils could be assigned to five minister-teachers, one hundred to each man, who would divide them into four sections of twenty-five each and meet them once a week for a full hour or more. Thus each minister might spend six to eight hours of his work week in the classroom. Or the preacher and his associate might better teach only two classes each a week — the one saving his time for sermon preparation and general pastoral work, the other concentrating on supervision and administration — while ordained teachers yet to be secured would take on eight to twelve hours of classroom work each.

Such a plan would be put into operation gradually, with the present two ministers teaching the high school classes and the lower grades continuing for the time being in the Sunday school. But as soon as qualified men and women minister-teachers are found, all pupils of school age would study under them at suitable intervals during the week.

But what about dislodging lay teachers, violating the principle that the minister is to be a " teacher of teachers "? [12] We shall be dealing with this issue at many points as we go along, but a quick answer is that laymen would serve as assistants, supervising lesson preparation, handling audio-visual aids, directing projects, dramatics, field trips and the like, provided the hour-a-week class might reasonably be expanded. In any event some would conduct tests and read pupil essays, and the few with rare gifts might teach. There need be no less use of lay people, only less misuse of them, a cessation of the present practice of co-ercing reluctant and unqualified laymen into trying to teach children accustomed to highly trained and com-petent professional teachers in the public schools. Instead of undertaking full responsibility for Biblical and doctrinal exposition, laymen would have the happy choice of using their particular interests and skills. Nor need there be un-due concern lest they prove more unavailable for these ministries during the week than on Sundays. Some might not, but others would welcome weekday assistanceships because Sunday is the one time when they are least in-clined to rush off to church work. And until the budget can be enlarged and women teachers secured — seminary grad-uates trained to teach — preschool and primary classes would continue under lay leadership. Moreover, the Sun-day school hour may well be retained on a different basis for all preadolescents with laymen directing church music, missionary activities, preparation for worship in the sanc-tuary, and use of the library.

Money is not the main difficulty at Suburban Church. Additional funds could be found at once to add one or two pastor-teachers at salaries comparable to those paid in local public and private schools. However, if tuition were charged, it is altogether likely that a community of this kind would value church education enough to encour-age children to attend classes more regularly than they have Sunday school. Both the superior merit of pastoral teaching and payment of a fee could be counted on to elicit interest. Parents who delay a family trip so that a child won't miss his weekly music lesson — a lesson already paid for — are likely to be the same parents disinclined to take the child out of town when he is due at his church class, particularly if that too has already been paid for. And what parent — given a choice between poor religious instruction at no fee and exceptional instruction at a cost comparable to that for music lessons — wouldn't prefer the latter for his child, even at a financial sacrifice? To be sure, Suburban Church cannot be taken either as typical or as a pattern for the rest of the country to follow. But it is one among hundreds in similar circumstances.

Let us suppose that only three hundred of the five hundred pupils respond to the new program. There are those who think it is time for Protestants to make a firm decision as to whether it is preferable to teach fewer people better, than to continue with superficial work among the swelling Sunday population. Actually, however, in the long run we are more likely to see even larger enrollments as a direct result of improved church teaching. Certainly the voluntary response of children and youth to meritorious teaching is not to be understimated.

Be that as it may, three hundred families, paying — let us say — sixty dollars each for an academic year, would mean an additional $18,000 for the church, enough to employ three new pastor-teachers at salaries comparable to those of schoolteachers in this particular community. Thus the needed staff of five ministers to teach five hundred prospective pupils is secured — provided, of course, competent people can be found. And no child would be deprived of attending classes because of lack of money, for surely churches can raise scholarship funds to meet their responsibility to all children. A further word must be said about fees. The question of whether to charge tuition undoubtedly will cause sharp differences of opinion.

Some will think Protestants would err if too many features of synagogue schools were adopted, and others will feel that a principle of stewardship is threatened by a pay-as-you-go plan. A compromise policy might well be adopted similar to Joseph Lancaster's humorous notice over the door of his first school, opened in London in 1801. The notice read: "All who will may send their children and have them educated freely, and those who do not wish to have education for nothing may pay for it if they please." [13]

2. We turn now to *City Church*, with a membership of around a thousand — about half of whom are active — and a Sunday school of about 150 children and adolescents. There are three ministers, one designated "minister of Christian education." Between eight and nine hundred people attend worship on a Sunday morning, the majority of whom are transients and other nonmembers attracted by able preaching and an impressive worship service. Of the members, the greater number do not live in the neighborhood but commute from the suburbs, in part because their forebears lived in the city and were members of this church. The annual budget of $150,000 is made possible by income on endowment, a sizable portion of which is allocated to salaries for the professional and lay staff, for the church operates on the conviction that a declining constituency calls for heavy expenditure for program. Therefore, Sunday school and released-time teachers, youth workers, and various activity leaders are paid for their services. Pastors and laymen alike are committed to the idea of good education and pupil enrollment has increased in recent years.

One of the pastors teaches the eighth grade for a few months each year, preparing pupils for church membership. During this time the regular Sunday school work for this age level is omitted. The other pastors teach adult classes at stated intervals and effort has been made to enlist college students taught by a seminary student. An interfaith weekday nursery class is provided as a service to the neighborhood. Nominal fees are charged but the cost is largely borne by the church. According to their wishes parents may receive individual and group guidance for the asking.

Here, too, is a church that has made a beginning toward effective education. It offers not the usual third-rate Sunday school program, but it has come to rest on a second-rate plateau, for most of its teachers are either college students — in training to become public-school teachers — or seminary students thinking only of a generalized ministry in the future. The former don't know the Bible and theology; the latter are not even teachers-in-training. So it is that we have another example — among the thousands over the country — of Protestantism's educational shortsightedness. This church's teaching program is deficient in comparison with the work done in a good public or private school. And it could provide genuine nurture, for it has the personnel and financial resources to do so.

In this and similar churches, pastor-teachers — theologically, Biblically, and educationally competent — ought to move at once toward fulfilling the demands of Luther, Calvin, Zwingli, Knox, and other Reformation leaders that Protestantism teach effectively. In his Yale lectures, delivered in 1888, H. Clay Trumbull observed that the Reformers " were alive to the importance of the revival of the primitive church-school idea," and added that " Luther went so far as to say that a clergyman was not fitted to be a preacher unless he had first been a teacher." [14] According to Trumbull — then the editor of *The Sunday School Times*

— the churches must teach if the "divinely commanded" task is to be carried out, must teach if "the best fruits of the Reformation are to be preserved and transmitted." And by teaching he meant "interlocutory teaching" — a method of conversation and dialogue.

Any city church that purposes to be more than a preaching station, and wonders how long it can survive and draw unchurched children off city streets in order to bring them up in Christian faith, may well reappraise its educational offering. That it will include on its staff pastor-teachers who can equal the best work of the rabbi in the synagogue and the priest in the Roman system, goes without saying. But the local church cannot do this alone; seminaries and graduate schools of religious education will first have to produce professional teachers.

3. Now let us look at a single-pastor town church. *Small-Town Church* is faced with manifold-housing, lay-leadership, and financial needs. The pastor conceives of his role as educator "as the most valid expression of the ministry," to use Prof. Samuel W. Blizzard's expression. This pastor thinks as does the one in twenty-five in Blizzard's study of 1,111 college- and seminary-trained men. He considers education "the major program of the church" whose "goal is that faith be communicated appropriately and comprehensively at every age level." He, like the few in the study, understands "the basic philosophy of education . . . the needs and abilities of children and young people, and possesses certain skills associated with an education program." [15]

Let it be clear that this pastor — so described and found by Blizzard in twenty-two denominations — lives in the flesh in the small-town church of which I am thinking. After three years of conducting leadership education, during which he has raised the standards of his Sunday school, there is no longer a problem of recruiting and training enough fairly capable teachers and officers to care for the 165 pupils and the twenty-one classes. Nevertheless, as an educator, he considers the work of his school inferior to that of the public school and — in his words — " would like . . . very much " to teach the youth himself. Before undertaking to schedule weekday classes, he thinks there is need for backing from a council of churches in order to secure a released-time plan. The fact that there is no junior or senior high school in the town bears on this problem, for the young people spend considerable time commuting to public schools in an adjoining community.

A realistic view of this and similar situations might make pastor-taught weekday classes conditional upon a released-time plan, but it is better for a church to avoid asking for either released or dismissed time. A working balance between the claims of school and church on the child's time need not curtail the academic program of the public schools. The balance we seek would seem to be one resulting from keeping certain extracurricular affairs within limits so that specified afterschool hours can be used by the churches. And in this particular case, we have a pastor whose interest and teaching ability give promise of attracting and holding youth to his classes on their own time. I must confess that I find distasteful the idea of using the public school's position to direct pupils into church classes. Nor can I reconcile the principle of church and state separation with any church's wish to borrow hours from school instruction. Granted that a sizable proportion of adolescents are in the public school only because they are required by law to be there, granted further that voluntary afterschool church classes — even with the best teacher on the job — will not initially draw as many pupils as the Sunday school, there is merit in superior teaching of the few instead of inferior teaching of the many. And in the long run, I anticipate that pastors' classes will not only provide more productive growth in Christ but will also enroll greater numbers of pupils. Obviously much depends on the pastor, as a person and as a teacher. But the true pastoral temperament, combined with the gift of teaching, is exactly what is needed to accomplish the educational mission of the church.

The pastor of another small-town church, who teaches three junior age classes on released time, contends that an 8:30 to 3:30 school day in his community — plus extracurricular activities held after school — and the transportation problem combine to rule out church classes on the children's time. Like Dr. Erwin L. Shaver — long an eloquent national leader of the released-time religious education movement — this pastor is convinced that where state law permits there is complete justification for churches' teaching on time released by the public school. In this instance I am happy to yield the point, both because I wish to avoid a legalistic stance and because the pastor is doing superior teaching in a community that clearly wants church classes arranged in co-operation with the schools. And this means the teaching is done only in the church building.

In a small church the pastor is in an enviable position to know and guide his people in Christian growth. And fortunate is the congregation whose children and parents have the benefit of their pastor's formal and informal week-by-week teaching.

The churches cited above cannot be taken as representative of all of American Protestantism with its multiplicity of types and governing conditions, nor can there be any abrupt shift from the Sunday school to inclusive pastoral teaching. Even if there were enough pastors qualified and desirous of teaching, enough money to enlarge professional staffs, and sufficient interest among the laity to warrant a decisive move toward church education, there would still be the Sunday school tradition to reckon with: the rooted custom of lay teaching and lay control of an organization that in some cases tends to rival the church rather than function as the church. The human disposition to grasp the familiar with renewed firmness the moment the new poses a threat has to be taken into account. I am under no illusion that it would be easy to enlarge the popular image of the ordained minister as preacher and pastor, or displace the image of the hatted-woman and big-brother type of layman as teacher and officer of the Sunday school. Nevertheless, many churches can begin to make the transition to genuine schools with pastor-teachers assisted by laymen and class hours scheduled on weekdays.

Picture the qualified teacher and the class setting. Like the teacher described by Dean Zeran, of Oregon State College,[16] the competent pastor-teacher "knows his subject field, the laws of learning, and then applies them to the teaching process." He "can motivate the student to accept the goal as his own." I would add that the pastor knows his pupils and their families and is their shepherd, a chief servant whose life and relationship with his people moves them Godward.

As for his pupils, they come to class expecting to work, to learn. Incidentally, they wear school clothes and these are more conducive to work than fancy dresses and creased trousers worn to Sunday school. The room itself is distinctly a classroom, larger and better equipped than the usual Sunday school room not only because this is what is needed but also because it is within the means of almost any church that abandons the policy of trying to house all pupils during a single hour. Instead of many unsuitable rooms there are a few good ones — used repeatedly during the week — containing open reference shelves, adequate cabinets for supplies, and proper desks. Handy storage space is provided for switching different sets of furniture back and forth to fit the needs of various classes.

Until pupils are willing and can find the time for outside preparation, a part of the hour is given to supervised study. Research and occasional projects definitely linked with the subject are included in the class procedure. There is little lecturing or reciting, even in higher grades; rather, there is much conversation about the subject being investigated. The teacher listens to his pupils, thus they are more disposed to listen to him. Teaching is largely a matter of prompting and dialogue. The best textbooks, reading books, and visual aids are used, available from any source.[17] Most books are supplied by the local church and remain its property; hence, they are hardback books, after the fashion of the Westminster and Seabury series. Some are purchased by the pupils for their own libraries.

Pupils are expected to range widely in their interests, according to their abilities. Not all classes need to be closely graded, but in general this system is followed. Drawing and painting by the younger children, essays and research by the older ones, are encouraged and due recognition is given to each pupil's progress. But the teacher is alert to prevent the class from becoming coldly intellectual, for he is pastor and friend who strives to transmute each class into a fellowship, a church in microcosm aware of its ties with the church universal. There is enjoyment here; there is also the ambivalence that attends every learning enterprise. Some fun, but no foolishness that makes the occasion trivial. Always the teacher sets the tone and he is a schoolmaster, albeit a warm person who represents the Master Teacher.

From grade to grade, year to year, one class to the next, pupils gain a sense of progression, of growth in faith and understanding of the Christian life and heritage. With achievement of this kind, summer classes become superfluous. Accordingly, the church class year matches the academic year of general education. A diploma is given upon satisfactory conclusion of the high school curriculum, and another one after two years of work paralleling that of a junior college. Graduates are ready for advanced collegiate or seminary study. Students who do not fulfill class requirements may qualify for a certificate of attendance.

◈

The proposal before us calls for a program of pastoral teaching in Protestant churches. The objective is to give children and youth more adequate nurture than that provided by Sunday schools and other agencies of the church. It is recognized that relatively few pastors now have either interest or ability necessary for this undertaking, but some churches have already made a beginning. If seminaries and denominations will proceed to create opinion favorable to this venture, theological students and churches may be counted on for support.

But what of parents' backing and pupils' willingness to attend church classes on a weekday? How realistic is it to expect high school or even junior high pupils to give place for religion in a week packed with athletics, bands and orchestras, homework, clubs, and earning money after school? These questions will be taken up in Chapter 6. They do indeed pose a problem. However, it can be solved — provided Protestants decide, under God, to put first things first, seeking God's Kingdom and his righteousness above all else. Not only in principle but in practice the church — the Christian community — must become the center of our children's lives; not the secular school and its exaggerated concern with sports and a plethora of activities, nor materialistic society and its deceptive values that cause adolescents to be preoccupied with earning money to spend for things they don't need.

Verily, the task before us is great, for it necessitates nothing less than a transformation of our values and rooted customs. By means of renewal of the church, in response to the working of the Holy Spirit, this transformation can take place.

5

The Pastor-Teacher and Christian Growth

COMPETENT minister-teachers, men and women, would provide better nurture than the Sunday schools can possibly do. We can honor the Sunday school movement for what it has meant in the past — a past less complex than our times with their exacting educational and theological demands on church teachers. But we fail to honor the cause of church education if we insist on subjecting relatively unprepared lay men and women and their pupils to a system decidedly inadequate for the task before us today. Here is an apt quotation from President Emeritus Cutten, of Colgate University: "A large number of persons on the faculties of our colleges and universities lack teaching ability and have no interest in the teaching function. Indeed, with the possible exception of the Sunday school, probably the poorest contemporary teaching is that to be found in our colleges." [18]

Whatever the reliability of Dr. Cutten's judgment of college teachers, the majority of Sunday school teachers *are* deficient both in knowledge of the Christian heritage and in teaching ability. Just how large a proportion are simply uninterested in the teaching function is an open question, but more important is the fact that Protestantism has persisted in relying on limited if not futile devices for preparing teachers. This is about as illogical as would be a decision to educate pastors by closing the seminaries and advising them to attend workshops, institutes, and occasional short-term lecture courses. And we might ask ourselves: What sort of preaching and pastoral ministry would we have were preachers to view their work as but one of many humanitarian services, often rendered under protest and almost always considered incidental to the main business of living? That pupils detect the general low regard adults have for teaching in the church is beyond dispute. It is little wonder, then, that few children respect the Sunday school or learn to know and love God above all else.

As difficult and radical as the task before us is, we Protestants simply have to enlist a new generation of pastors committed to preparing themselves for classroom teaching.

Let us visualize church classes for children and youth taught by interested and capable ministers at stated periods during the week. These men and women would view teaching as no less important than preaching and would prepare themselves for classroom work with the same care used in preparation of the best sermons. They would strive to make church teaching equal to or better than that to which their pupils are accustomed in general education. The churches would back them, knowing that it is unrealistic to expect any but the most exceptional laymen to be as well equipped as pastors in Bible, theology, church history, and the rest. However, long before seminary graduates are ready to teach, there will have to come into being a new conception of the pastor's work and the significance of nurture for redemption of youth and adults. To this end official policy by the denominations and seminaries must first give form and substance to the idea of pastoral teaching.

In Chapter 4 we considered what the church ought to try to accomplish with students. We observed that commitment to Christ and the acquisition of knowledge are our main goals. In this chapter we address ourselves to the teacher's relationship to his pupils and their families, and open up the question of what the seminary must do to prepare men and women for church teaching.

Although Protestants are not without precedent for including teaching in the work of the pastor, so far as I have been able to determine, ordination rites in denominations that mention teaching refer mainly to pulpit instruction. It was the custom of early Congregationalists to ordain and install one man as pastor and another as teacher, the latter being charged with expounding doctrine. In colonial America, however, a church could not afford two ministers and soon it came about that a man was chosen as pastor and teacher,[19] a custom that has continued to the present. Not only in New England but elsewhere the preacher was often also a schoolmaster. Indeed, schools and colleges and Protestantism grew up together in this country. But the past century has seen a widening of the breach between popular education and the churches. While tax-supported schools have established skilled professional instructional staffs, Protestant churches — unlike Judaism and Roman Catholicism — have tried to convince themselves that lay staffs can carry on effective teaching. This is not so.

The time has come for us to have fully qualified teachers for our children. And I know of no denomination that maintains that a pastor is called to minister only to adults. A child or adolescent no less than an adult deserves to have direct and very personal contact with his minister. Children are eager for recognition and support by the pastor, not superficially but at a genuine pastoral level. They stand ready to respond to him, if he proves that he has an affinity for them, for as we have already noted they want a significant person — to use the current phrase — to relate to, to admire, to look up to. More often than adults perhaps, they are quick to identify themselves with a person of recognized merit. For those in middle childhood and adolescence, a man of God is needed; and for many younger children, a woman of God.

Let this be emphasized. God, the church, and basic needs of the young come to focus in the pastor, a principal mediator of Christian growth. The pastor-teacher who can relate himself to his pupils is exactly what Protestantism must provide if spiritual integrity is to characterize boys and girls.

Children at all ages have deep longing to be known, listened to, understood, and guided — by someone, and by the someone who stands in peculiar relationship to God. The worthy pastor-teacher can give the child stability with which to cope with personal fears and perplexities in a rudderless society and a home that like as not is devoid of God's grace. The young need human models and will have them one way or another. As the research of Dr. Richard V. McCann suggests,[20] personality development requires admiration of another, one to whom the child looks not only in early years but also in later childhood for clues in living, valuing, becoming mature, experiencing salvation. This holds true for the child from the best home and the worst, for the child from the former needs also an estimable model outside the family, and the child from the latter more acutely needs a good model. Perhaps the church has conformed too much to the world precisely because its children and youth have had inadequate relationships with the minister.

A proper relationship between the child and the minister of Christ is achieved in the measure that the pastor *is* himself, man of God, embodiment of Christian grace and knowledge, as such enabling the child to become what he was created to be: also man of God, therefore redeemed. Beyond acquisition of knowledge, this relationship — established in acceptance, companionship, love — is utterly different from the surface relationships now existing between pastor and children in most churches.

Have we not overlooked the significance of a child's preoccupation with teachers? Listen to the young talk among themselves, rating schoolteachers, revealing their adoration for some, resistance to others, hatred for a few. But all teachers are considered persons to be reckoned with, for the child knows his fate hinges on them. Discerning in his judgment, the child is happy when he can praise the teacher, most happy when he has one whose personal standards and professional ability are above reproach. In sum, a child not only wants to be admired, but also to admire.

Is it not cause for lamentation that a pastor sometimes caught up in exaltation in delivery of a powerful sermon, seldom knows similar exaltation in a teaching experience? True, the gift of teaching is rare, especially so among men whose entire orientation is to proclamation rather than to dialogue and critical inquiry shared by a class. Nevertheless, when pastors become teachers, they will discover depths and heights unknown in their adult world, for the child world is marked by quickness to trust, to give loyalty and affectionate response to a respected mentor.

High on the list of a child's needs today is the perennial need to learn right from wrong. The shepherd may confidently be expected to have firmer standards than most of his flock, truer moral and ethical perception, more valid spiritual insights concerning what God requires of child and man. Moral authority and religious sanction are the pastor's province as is not ordinarily the case with parents and schoolteachers. This is no plea for clergymen to dispense moralisms; rather it is a call for relationship between pastor and children wherein teaching-learning proceeds by clear and worthy example, and by conversation that clarifies issues of Christian belief and conduct. Children from the best as well as the worst homes stand in need of coming to terms with valid authority, for the authority of contemporary life is of dubious quality, and the authority of God in Christ so far removed from many children and church families as to be wholly alien. Who better than the pastor-teacher, in an effective relationship with children, can provide authoritative guidance and church teaching requisite for personal faith and conduct?

Emmanuel Mounier wisely points out that in dealing with the child " one must mingle grace with discipline, relaxation with effort." [21] This suggests the combination of qualities essential for the pastor in classroom and parish, in his relations with the young. At its finest, the class becomes an occasion for pastor and children to grow together in Christ by partaking of the *agapē* nature of the church, an experience familiar to pastors who have had exalted spiritual moments with the confirmation or church membership classes.

It cannot be said too often that the pastor's teaching task is larger than that of instruction, for it includes the sort of guidance of persons that gives greatest promise of their nurture in Christ. Nurture, of course, means education; and education for Christian living depends on experiences fostered within the household of faith, the church. These experiences produce knowledge, understanding, and growth of the person in the measure that they are ordered and illuminated by a thoroughly competent teacher. The relationships thus achieved are the ground from which growth in Christ is realized. Born in the image of God, each individual is endowed with capacity to fulfill his godly nature. But fulfillment requires nurture through fellowship.[22] The church, as the body of Christ, is the habitat of the Holy Spirit, the matrix essential for the growth of persons in grace and knowledge of God as revealed in Jesus Christ. This growth signifies that a person is being educated for Christian living. It is neither growth for growth's sake, nor merely a matter of collecting information, finding wisdom, developing skills for effective living. Christian growth does entail knowledge in general and knowledge of Christianity in particular; and nurture in Christ may be expected to lead the growing person to wisdom, cause him to perform sundry tasks skillfully, and stimulate him to live effectively on a personal and social level.

Beyond the imparting of information the task of the pastor-teacher is one of engendering understanding so that persons in their freedom may decide to be Christian, and having decided, may grow in Christian grace. Christian growth is always a becoming, a process that starts at birth and continues while life is consciously maintained. How is it accomplished?

Let us recall what takes place during the growth process in which the human individual comes to be a person. The human infant is born with capacities to become a person.

At birth the infant possesses only the raw materials of personality. He belongs to the human species, but he becomes a person only if he has the care of humans to whom he will respond appropriately as he interacts with them. It is often pointed out that a child needs the nourishing matrix of a loving family in order to develop his personality. Leave his upbringing to a wolf mother and he will run on all fours, eat and snarl like a wolf, be unable to talk, remain subhuman. There are numerous studies that attest to the child's dependence on his early human environment for gaining human personality. Furthermore, the native intelligence and unique potential of the child are decisively affected by the quality of the human and cultural environment in which he lives. His inherent temperament, neuromuscular system, and native intelligence merely give promise of his development as a human being, for, in infancy, he bears but the image of the human. And that image is distorted and lost unless the infant is permitted to interact with humans. He not only needs persons but utterly depends on them to enable him to realize his own human image. This theory strengthens the viewpoint that man is created to live in social relations, in community. To live on the human level is to be in community.

The infant, then, learns to be a person by living in suitable relation with persons. Learning involves levels of growth and the unique responses that the child, as an organism, makes to the human and cultural environment. Infants deprived of mothering, though receiving good physical care, become listless, tense, un-co-operative, lose weight, and may evidence hostility.[23] A child needs loving care both to be human and to learn to love. Unless from infancy onward he is accepted, fondled, given consistent love, he does not learn to trust persons. Thus his growth is arrested. He learns mistrust and, accordingly, is unfitted to grow up as a co-operative human being capable of effective relations with his fellows.

During the years one to five the personality is coming into being. These are the years during which the child imitates others around him and identifies with parents, or parent substitutes. Both his growth and his learning to be a person depend on his having persons about him. His emerging personality is certainly the product of his interaction with environment, and the human environment is more significant than the material environment. What the child becomes is largely up to parents, the sort of persons they are.

But the child is also drawing sustenance for his growth from society: the neighborhood, the school, the community. Because he is fundamentally a social being he is dependent upon his fellows as he relates to them, learning from them, gaining his growth in conduct and thought and value from them. Happily he is not wholly subject to his human environment. Environment is not the sole determinant of what a given person is to be, for each person is unique, created to become himself. Nonetheless, he gains the self only as he is interrelated with persons. In short, it is in social relations that one learns to be a personality. Growth of the organism, alone, does not bring about a condition of being a good citizen, a worthy member of society. In addition, both informal and formal learning are necessary.

Life itself is a learning experience and so long as we live we can learn. Though effective learning depends partly on youth and a healthy state of the organism, one not only can keep on learning but needs to do so, regardless of age and health. Various institutions are established to

ensure certain kinds of learning. In America we have public and other schools for the purpose of educating the
young for democratic citizenship. Due to the lengthened
life span of our citizens and their increasing desire to keep
on learning, numerous provisions are made for adult learning on a more formal and systematized basis than can be
provided by the individual on his own, as he learns from
life experiences.

In sum, one learns to be a person. His learning is
achieved as his unique capacities interact with the humans
about him. What he learns, what he becomes, is the product of native gifts of his maturing organism in dynamic
relations with human environment. Habits, attitudes, values of whatever kind, stem from relations provided by the
society in which one lives, grows, and learns. A totalitarian
society and its culture tend to produce authoritarian personalities. A democracy and its culture tend to produce
persons valuing and practicing freedom. I say " tend," for
there is within any society great variability among persons, precisely because each individual is unique, with his
own peculiar capacities and purposes. What he is to become is always largely up to him.

Now if the human individual becomes a person by virtue
of growing and learning within a human community, it is
also true that the Christian becomes what he is by growing
and learning within the Christian community. As God is
in Christ and Christ is in the church, so persons in Christian community are in Christ, and in one another. In fellowship persons interact, affect one another for good or
ill, build one another up or tear one another down. If the
fellowship is governed by forbearance and love, its members are not only nurtured by experiencing the meaning
of brotherliness but are also enabled to grow in grace.

The church is a fellowship of forgiving and forgiven sinners who receive among themselves God's gift of himself through Christ.

By God's grace, by his release of power among persons in Christian relationships, personal and corporate growth takes place. Thus persons grow in grace. This growth is due to the presence of the Living God in the life of the church. Not merely humans are interacting with one another, but individuals are encountering God in Christ. Within the encounter more than knowledge about God is learned; the Person is experienced by persons. This experience changes people, causes them to think and feel differently, to become different. God's holiness flows into the worshiping community and the Spirit's redemptive work is accomplished in love and judgment. Adults and youth are moved to repentance, perceiving their lack of wholeness over against God's holiness, knowing themselves evil in the sight of God. His grace, as enabling power, is given to the church so that the individual may draw upon it, appropriate it for his basic need to live redemptively, and use it to express a new dimension of human personality. In a state of grace the individual both comes to himself — returns to and fulfills the image of God in which he was created — and comes to God, by coming to his fellows in Christ. In love he comes, knowing he is the recipient of unmerited love from his fellows and from God.

In Christian fellowship the individual experiences God, and this experience assures growth in grace no less than growth in the knowledge of God revealed in Christ. Even as little children are sensitive to emotional tones within the kinship family, they are also sensitive to Christian love within the family of God, the church. All who minister to nursery children, in home and church, are called to bear in themselves the image of Christ so that children may be partakers of Christian love. All teachers working with all age levels both informally and formally, are called to practice the Protestant principle of the mutual ministry of believers. Each one, says Luther, " should become as it were a Christ to the other, that . . . Christ may be the same in all." [24] This is mutuality requisite for Christian teaching and learning.

But the developing person is not ultimately bound by the limitations of associates nor foreordained to be but a duplication of them, for the dynamic self normally grows beyond the stages of mere imitation and identification and reflects its own uniqueness under God. Nevertheless, it is sobering and humbling to realize that just as we adults have selected and appropriated qualities, attitudes, values, faiths derived from persons with whom we have identified, so the young and the more impressionable adults who identify with us are largely becoming like us. If Christ is in us, they incorporate him. If we are evil, they incorporate evil.

Even as all humans learn from one another and come to themselves only as they are related to community, so Christians learn from one another and come to fulfillment of themselves within Christian community. Because Christ is in his church and, in truth, is everywhere that two or three are gathered in his name, Christian personality is achieved in human interaction. Being what the psychologist calls an energy system, and what the Christian calls a person empowered by God's love, one inevitably exerts forces that influence another. Humans release power that impinges upon one another. As Christians they give affection to one another, and the product of this affection is Christian love transcending anyone's merit viewed separately. In the community of love persons learn to be reconciled to one another and hence to God. They gain a new quality of life, for they are growing in grace. This growth is precisely nurture in Christ, an educative experience that teaches the oldest among us that learning to be Christian is continuous with life. Each stage of life calls for the unlearning of old habits, wrong attitudes, false values, inadequate faiths. Love is never pure, motives are always mixed, evil is subtle and alluring. The pastor, the senior deacon, the dedicated parent, the least selfish child, and the most idealistic youth, all — because of pride — suffer alienation from God. In love we are to guide our fellows back to atonement with God. In patience, long-suffering kindness, meekness, and outgoing love we are to admonish one another — judge one another, if you please, as God is our Judge — and be the means for redeeming one another.

Nurture by means of Christian community, however, is general and somewhat diffuse. It needs complementing by the teaching of particular bodies of knowledge. And the mutual ministry of believers is a stronger ministry when the pastor assumes major responsibility for giving direct and systematic instruction and personal guidance of growing individuals.

As educator, the pastor also enters into relationship with the families of his pupils, for he recognizes the primacy of the home for nurturing persons in Christian faith. Moreover, he is sensitive to adult longing for relationship wherein the sense of meaninglessness pervading human lives is dispelled. Let me mention two dominant but rather inarticulate desires that I believe many people have. They are: desire for a family physician to blot out one's depersonalizing and humiliating experiences when visiting clinics and their squadrons of specialists with machines, charts, and statistical procedures; and desire for a pastor who is a shepherd in time of joy and sorrow, at birth and at death. Pastors err who choose program promotion to the exclusion of pastoral visits; who turn the church study into a counselor's office, imitating psychiatrists; who for any reason abandon pastoral contacts with the excuse that nowadays people don't want a clergyman bothering them. On the contrary, men and women today, as always, want to be known, to be seen whole, and to receive pastoral attention. They are sick of being fragmented by modern life, repulsed by being shunted from specialist to specialist, from superficial and impersonal interview to more of the same. Though they may not realize it, for themselves and their children they yearn for a living, rallying center embodied in the man of God who can make himself available to them, entering into their lives, guiding them through his life into oneness with the Christ of God.

Can this be true? Is it right to contend that an urbanized civilization absorbed in economic security, in pleasurable pursuits, in avoiding involvement with neighbor and the world, actually desires communion with a pastor and his God — a God who inevitably makes disturbing demands? I think it is true. I assert it is true, for man's basic need is for community and communion — precisely those experiences negated by the current mode of existence.

The anonymity of the city, the frenetic pace of suburbia, the imposing of mechanized bigness and cultural conformity even on rural America, cheapen the human order and diminish the individual and his family. Mediocrity, sameness, timidity, mar us and we are stamped " Standardized Products," things. Our life is shallow; our selves, empty; for we — in the church and outside it — have vainly sought to fill ourselves with busyness, motion, things, all the while slipping into the toils of an other-directed society. But now it is clear that the more we have poured even good things and good activities into ourselves the emptier we have become. Those within the church though presumably fed, hunger; though looking up to see the shepherd, they see him not — because he is swallowed up in playing organization man running a church that is no church.

Happily there are young men graduating from our seminaries resolved to lead their flocks into becoming the church, the household of God against which the hell of the world shall not prevail. Certain gifted young pastors come to mind, men whose eyes are fixed on the small, intimate, face-to-face flock, avoiding the large institution sometimes mistaken for a church. At once I hasten to explain that I do not equate a small parish with a colony of God on an alien continent of big churches. Bigness of the institution does not necessarily make estrangement from God inevitable. Both in the small and the large flock the sheep can hear the shepherd, can know, and be known by, him — provided he and they so arrange his task that he reaches them where they live, in their families.

At risk of repetition, I am again making the suggestion that a pastor can minister at an effective level to the needs of 50 to a 100 families, a congregation of from 250 to 400 persons, sharing family life with them, teaching classes of children, youth, and parents. If there are more than 100 to 125 school age children in the church, his teaching load might prove too heavy. Hence it would be better for him to include only older children and adolescents in his classes. Six hours a week spent in teaching, eight to ten hours for class preparation and follow-up with individual pupils, may reasonably occupy him. As preacher he needs at least eight to twelve hours to work on his sermon, deliver it, and conduct public worship. This totals a maximum of twenty-eight hours of his work week. Add about ten hours for pastoral calls, allow another ten for funerals, weddings, board and committee meetings, and sufficient time is left from a forty-eight-hour-week for meditation, study, recreation, and his own family's affairs. And administrative tasks? Let there be less of them — assuredly so to the extent that on analysis it is found that the pastor's administrative function has become like that of the business executive. A new conception of leadership training would prepare laymen to assume much of the administrative and promotional work now carried by the minister, thus freeing him to be pastor and teacher.

To be sure, there are other demands made on the pastor's time — notably by denominational, interdenominational, and civic enterprises. These create problems to which we shall return in the next chapter.

By devoting himself to teaching the young, the pastor may find the way opening for a more fruitful kind of home call in which he talks over individual needs and abilities and gives informal guidance to the family group. What is paramount is not so much the substance of these conversations as the relationship formed between family and pastor. Admittedly, most times only the mother and perhaps a small child are at home when the pastor calls, but visits can be made at hours when the father and the rest of the family are present. In any event, in view of the fact that members of the modern family tend to go their separate ways, much preliminary work needs to be done with individuals before a great number of families are ready as a group for a visit and conference with the pastor. Meantime pastoral calls are quite in order, even though made to but one or two persons.

Young couples contemplating marriage need the pastor's guidance. And this I see not in terms of so-called marriage counseling — at stated periods in a church office — so much as in terms of three people in friendly, earnest conversation, carried on in the parsonage living room or possibly in the living room in the prospective bride's home. In either setting the three are to be left strictly to themselves for all or part of the conversation. Instead of professionalized marriage counseling, therefore, informality and friendship mark the occasion, an occasion improved by coffee and cookies with the pastor as host in his home or the bride-to-be as hostess in her parents' home.

After marriage the couple find the pastor's concern issuing in guidance anticipating the birth of children. Thus young parents are prepared to covenant with the church to nurture the child in Christian love and faith. The growing family is rooted in the worshiping community and no matter what trouble and estrangement may come the pastor and the ministering community are there to sustain both children and parents. Whether healing or divorce follows, persons are supported, even greater love being given when sin and suffering rend the family group. Always both pastor and ministering community remember that they are to give themselves first to the lost, like the Great Physician, concerning themselves more with the sick than with those who are well. Not condemnation of persons but the overcoming of sin is the aim of the spiritual mentor of family life, especially so because strained and broken family relationships are so prevalent in our society.

Through an educational and personal ministry of this sort, children and parents are prepared for family worship services of a quality not generally achieved in the churches. Kinship families closely linked with the pastor are ready now to enter into the life of the church family, and persons united in Christ are joined to one another in the fellowship of grace. Thereby the worshiping community comes into being, and persons divided within themselves, alienated from one another and from God, are made whole, redeemed.

We turn next to look briefly at the church served by two or more pastors. The same kind of strategy used in the small church for effecting close relations between pastor and people is suitable for the large church. Let us suppose that a church has a pastor-teacher for every fifty to a hundred families comprising it. A division of labor enables each man to serve the families of the children enrolled in his classes, but parishioners do not have to confine themselves to their particular pastor; all hear the preacher, and any family is free to ask any one of the pastors to perform a marriage or render some other service. Even so it is the responsibility of the pastor assigned to a given section of the local church to provide his flock with complete pastoral care, despite considerable overlapping where there are large families with children studying under different men.

Although their respective functions are clearly defined, the pastors operate as a closely knit staff, " in honor preferring one another," by grace able to permit members of the church to show whatever preferences they may. The man whose name appears at the top of the staff is usually the preacher and — though not called that — also chief of staff. There is no assistant pastor, no director of education. The pastors think of themselves as colleagues, teachers and servants whose additional duties are designated by the church by such terms as " chairman of church life " to indicate lay administrative development and "program

chairman" to indicate missionary and evangelistic outreach. In some situations a layman might well be em-
ployed to raise the budget and manage the general business of the church, thereby conserving the pastors' strength
for their more basic responsibilities.

The heart of the matter before us is this: the establishing of a pastoral teaching ministry in Protestant churches.
Toward this goal less difficulty may be encountered with
laymen than with pastors, seminary students, and the
seminaries themselves. The one in twenty-five pastors
Professor Blizzard found who views education as central
in the ministerial task very likely does not represent the
country at large. I suspect that hardly one in a hundred
Protestant pastors in the United States thinks so highly of
education. Even the eleven hundred men Blizzard studied
had in mind not the role of classroom teacher so much as
that of educational administrator. One need only spend
some time on a seminary campus to know the extent to
which students ignore or disclaim the teaching program
of the churches. I once asked a class of twenty-three men
how many of them were interested in teaching. About half
raised their hands. I expressed surprise and amended, " I
mean teaching in the church." Then I wasn't surprised —
but the class was, for jaws dropped at sudden realization
that teaching could possibly refer to anything but college
teaching. And this particular class had just spent about
two months considering the educational work of the local
church! Their reaction, of course, reflects none too favor-
ably on the instructor; but it also reflects the seminarian's
predisposition to limit his role to preaching and pastoral
care. But then the seminaries have given students no vision
of pastoral teaching.

One learns to teach by teaching, under guidance, di-

rected and inspired by a master teacher in a fruitful classroom situation. To this calling seminary students will
surely turn when churches, colleges, and seminaries —
stimulated by denominational commissions on the ministry
— chart the way. I am encouraged to believe that 20 to 40
per cent of able seminary students are normally attracted
by teaching. True, they generally think only of college
posts but they can develop interest in church teaching.
The fact is that there is no higher calling, no greater need;
in a sense, systematic church teaching of children demands
greater professional competence than college teaching,
for the most satisfactory contemporary teaching in America — according to Sidney Hook [25] — is not found in the
colleges but in elementary and secondary schools. If this
be true, then pastor-teachers are challenged to perform at
least as well as the best teachers in America, realizing that
pupils are inevitably comparing them with their teachers
in general education.

◈

To summarize the argument thus far, Protestants need
church education carried on during the week by pastors
who are Biblically, theologically, and educationally competent. Beyond knowledge of the Christian heritage, experience with Christ is the goal as teacher, pupils, and
their families enter into a growing relationship. A child
wants to know, and to be known by, his pastor. He and
his parents will respect significant teaching; therefore,
support it. The program of formal church education will
use laymen as class assistants and directors of projects,
and informal nurture will certainly involve not fewer but
more laymen, for the Christian community — living its
life in church and family — is the matrix in which persons
become members one of another, learning of God.

Church education calls for a new conception of the pastor's role, a realignment of tasks resulting in the laymen's carrying more of the promotional and business enterprises of the church, thus freeing the pastor to use to the full his special gifts as minister and teacher. Fewer and larger classrooms, used repeatedly during the week, will induce a more satisfactory educational architecture, a more faithful discharge of stewardship responsibility, a conserving of funds to employ pastor-teachers as needed. And an intensive teaching and pastoral ministry to individuals and families can truly nurture persons in the grace and knowledge of our Lord and his gospel.

6

Overcoming Obstacles

HOWEVER APPEALING the idea of establishing church education of high calibre, there are obstacles to pastor-taught classes, some of which have already been touched upon. Major obstacles include: (1) the belief that pastors cannot or should not learn to teach; (2) skepticism about the possibility and suitability of pastors' finding time for teaching; (3) the problem of sufficient personnel in view of the shortage of ordained ministers; (4) the assumption that church classes are secondary in importance to just about everything else in the child's life; and (5) the contemporary doctrine that the church as a whole is the proper and sufficient educator. We now examine these in the order given.

There are those who believe quite firmly that parsons cannot or should not learn to teach, and that if they did they would be driving a wider wedge between themselves and a laity. This viewpoint merits reflection.

Perhaps the main reason for skepticism about pastors' becoming teachers stems from the image of inflexible, excessively didactic men whose very manner, when they enter a room in which people have been talking freely, causes sudden silence. On the other hand, there seems to be cause for thinking that ministerial pontification is declining. True, teaching as guidance is alien to the authoritarian personality, whether clerical or lay, and authoritarianism may remain to motivate a pastor long after he has expunged himself of any tendency to pontificate. The problem with respect to teaching is very like the problem of preaching. In both instances it is essential that a man speak with authority, yet not authoritarianism. But teaching particularly requires great patience and willingness to explore pertinent issues, and some pastors have extreme difficulty in modulating proclamation to the mood and pace of the classroom. Though temperamentally disposed to tell people what is what, in the classroom the pastor simply must restrain himself and help pupils discover and appropriate the meaning and truth of the gospel. If he fails to realize that learners seldom respond to the short cut of sheer ex-cathedra utterance, then the last stage of the teaching — church education — may be worse than the first, the Sunday school.

Now if the art of teaching escapes the rigid preacher, it is not to be thought of as alien to true shepherds. Just how far seminarians can be led toward preparing themselves as church teachers cannot be known until this phase of ministerial education is given due attention. Though neither preachers nor teachers are made in the seminary, proper seminary training can improve their performance; and doubtlessly such men will be much in demand in the future. For once familiar with the idea of church education, churches will be eager to secure pastor-teachers. In the interim, those who say that pastors cannot teach are reminded that up to the present time it has hardly occurred to the seminaries to get them ready for teaching.

More serious is the argument that the teaching role is to be avoided by the pastor because it pre-empts the work of lay folk and thus removes the clergy one step farther from them. Not so; but this issue needs illumination. First, it should be reiterated that the qualified church teacher is more than likely to be one who has had a theological education. Not his office as an ordained minister but his education and availability extend to him, rather than to laymen, the call to teach. Again, not that the professional minister is invariably more competent than the exceptional layman in teaching but that the former has greater opportunity both to equip himself to teach and to combine this function with pastoral work — work that goes hand in hand with guidance of pupils and their families. In principle, all baptized churchmen are ministers, servants possessing varieties of gifts to be used — according to their respective aptitudes — in witnessing to the saving gospel. No one is to be denied rendering any service of which he is capable. By virtue of ability and the will of the Christian fellowship, any layman may in principle occasionally preach, administer the sacraments, engage in evangelism, teach. So much for the doctrine of the priesthood of all believers. However, for the sake of order and appropriateness, most communions choose to designate some to serve the church "full time," freeing them from occupations other than pastoral work. Not so much by ethical merit or by spiritual superiority — though these are generally imputed to the parson despite his too being a sinner — is one "set aside" for a pastoral ministry, as by the practical need of the church for this sort of concentrated service. At one end of the scale the Mormons and the Quakers — examples of communions having no ordained ministry — seem closer to the Protestant doctrines of the mutual ministry of believers; and at the other end of the scale, a communion controlled by a highly ordered polity seems closer to the New Testament principle that holds that Christ's " gifts were that some should be apostles, some prophets, some evangelists, some pastors and teachers " (Eph. 4:11).

It is interesting to note that the conjunction here links the pastoral office with teaching, which bespeaks the appropriateness of pastors' engaging in teaching. Those who are more priestly than pastoral will disagree, judging by the fact that the strongest objection thus far heard to church education has come from persons not of congregational orientation but episcopal. This is quite understandable, though the basis given is ironical: that for pastors to teach increases the separation between laymen and clergymen. Perhaps I may be pardoned if I suggest that the way to avoid separation is to minimize the priestly office and for all ministers, laymen included, to be deacons — which, being servants of God, they are.

Perhaps far more clergymen than is generally realized would welcome having a group of lay advisers say to them that teaching merits priority over much of the administrative, denominational, and civic work hitherto levying claims on the pastor. Indeed, one of the most fruitful undertakings that could be carried out by laymen and their pastor would be that of enumerating and classifying the sundry pastoral duties, this preparatory to realigning duties. Such a process would at least prove informative and might well eventuate in eliminating many existing responsibilities in favor of a richer and more concentrated pastoral and teaching ministry. Laymen will need to exercise caution lest they push a pastor into teaching before he is ready for it, and pastors will have to trust the Protestant principle of mutual ministry through which policy is arrived at by consensus of laity and clergy. Together they should find a way to use the pastor's training and talents with greater wisdom than in the recent past. Do not too many pastors spend too many days in local and area committee and board meetings? Are not too many hours given to counseling too few individuals — in what could be a good and needed ministry but is beginning to look dangerously like a fad? By taking thought, and with their laymen sharpening the pastoral role, ordained ministers can begin to draw on their years of education to fulfill their mission as pastors, preachers, teachers.

The statement "The minister's time is not his own," though true to some extent, is also misleading. In this connection it is well to recall that many physicians teach as well as practice medicine, for the most part managing to keep regular teaching hours. Even so, when pastor and people understand that only in actual emergencies is it permissible to call the teacher away from his classes, it will prove quite possible for a parish to benefit by pastor-taught classes. And when illnesses, funerals, and weddings multiply — disrupting the suggested forty-eight-hour week of the pastor — it will be remembered that normally there are more weeks when his time is his own to a greater degree. Despite claims to the contrary, on examination I believe it will be found that a pastor has sufficient time to teach a few hours a week, and prepare for his classes, without taxing himself unduly or curtailing other important pastoral functions. Some pastors may avoid regular teaching not because they do not have the time for it (or the potential ability) but because they prefer simpler tasks. But instead of trying to force them to bestir themselves, laymen will be advised to arouse churches and seminaries to the need for producing a new and different generation of pastor-teachers. To this end financial and educational improvements will have to be made in churches and seminaries alike.

Meantime, a church committee searching for a pastor should bear in mind the desirability — yea, the need — of selecting a man fully committed to teaching as a phase of his wider pastoral ministry. And when laymen and theological professors face their respective responsibilities for preparing minister-teachers, the ranks of the few now available will be enlarged to the advantage of the churches. It cannot be overemphasized that we have all been thoughtless, if not misguided, in so far as a pastor's work is concerned. Laymen have looked in vain to clergymen for valid interpretation of the pastoral role; clergymen have looked to the seminaries; seminaries have looked to the churches whereupon — finding the looking circular — the churches have turned their attention to society; hence, the managerial, executive pattern taken from business, widely adopted by parsons and grafted on to what in recent times seems to be a pattern drawn from the psychiatrist or clinical psychologist. It is to counteract our general drift and neglect that the principal tasks of the shepherd of the flock are defined in terms of pastor, preacher, teacher. And, let it be added, we are considering not alone an argument for pastors' teaching but for their subsuming under their calling as shepherd of the flock only those roles which are truly organic to their calling. At the same time, both pastors and laymen need to perceive that in the measure that pastoral teaching may increase, other ministries by laymen will also have to increase, notably those of administering the many affairs of the modern church.

Allied with the problem of providing time for the pastor to teach is the long-range question about the suitability of his doing so, particularly in the later years of his ministry. Although it may be somewhat premature to discuss this aspect of the problem, nevertheless, we should note that it is a mistake to assume that only young men and women make good teachers of children and adolescents. Depending on his interest, proficiency, and vitality, a pastor — like many teachers in elementary and high schools — might continue in the classroom until the age of retirement. Or, as he grows older and his physical energies decline, the church may bring in a younger colleague to take over the teaching, just as is customary when an aging pastor requires a general assistant.

A group of laymen about to inaugurate church education will be on sound grounds if the problem of ministerial continuity is faced squarely. Some people doubt the justification for launching a pastoral teaching program because so many pastors abide only briefly in a parish. The reasoning here is that even though a man were to stay long enough in a given parish to build up a thorough educational piece of work, the chances would be small for finding a successor capable of the same kind of work. And yet it seems reasonable to expect pastor-teachers to remain in churches longer than other pastors, simply because a church that cares enough for the quality of pastor-people relations and teaching about which we are thinking in these pages is likely to be a community of believers growing in Christ. In such a church there is no ceiling on what a pastor can accomplish, and — more to the point — there is infinitely less reason for him or the congregation to terminate their connection in order to advance either the cause of Christ or themselves.

But — a student of mine points out — in our mobile society not only parsons but also parishioners are wont to migrate from church to church, from community to community. What of children and their families, accustomed to well-conducted, minister-taught classes, who may find themselves in a new community where only inferior education is offered in the churches? The thought behind this question appears to be that until most parishes are ready to adopt church education, a parish here or a parish there — committed to the best education possible — would be rendering its people a disservice by exposing them to meritorious teaching. It is as though people deficient in diet were given good food for a time, only to have to move on and be deprived again. And this time they are different in expectation and demand because they have at least had a taste of proper nourishment. The question then becomes, Is their last condition worse than the first? Not necessarily, I think, for they can give themselves to the job of providing themselves with food like that which they enjoyed briefly. So, also, children and parents who have had some experience with church education and who then moved to a community where it is unavailable can stimulate their new parish to establish church education. Lest this be taken as a mere belaboring of the obvious, let it be given point by emphasizing that the designing of church education for any parish is the responsibility of laymen no less than clergymen.

The problem of securing personnel for handling all ages of children may at first seem insoluble. Let us suppose that a church with a suitable number of children for one minister to teach is seeking a pastor. Is the church to revert to something of the situation that long prevailed in the one-room, single-teacher public school, and to expect its pastor to be versatile enough to teach both young children and adolescents? I have suggested that fifth-grade pupils and older pupils may be taught by the pastor while younger pupils remain with lay leaders for the Sunday school hour. To some people this insinuates that good teaching is not equally important for all ages. Not so, and I shall deal presently with pastoral teaching of children under ten. But on the other hand, most pastor-teachers are likely to be better suited to older classes. Exacting enough is an age range from ten and up! And of course not all pastors will be uniformly capable with junior, junior high, senior high, and older students. Indeed, like teachers in general education, pastor-teachers will but in exceptional cases move with ease from age level to age level and from subject to subject. What then?

Three recommendations are in order. First, a church of from fifty to one hundred families should look for one of the few pastors in the country who is presently capable of teaching juniors, adolescents, and adults with equal facility. A man competent with only one of these age levels is not for the small church. Second, larger churches, formerly satisfied with just one pastor — who cannot possibly teach and minister personally to the many families of the parish — should count the financial cost of adequate personnel and then set about securing it. Yet this proposal runs up against the oft-reported shortage of seminary graduates — men and women with *ordinary* ministerial training — a fact that further complicates the problem of securing men capable of the teaching and pastoral work herein called for. In this respect it is fortunate that the churches of the country will not be making a unison demand for minister-teachers; this being true, the seminaries will have some years in which to recruit and prepare candidates for the new kind of ministry needed. Third, numbers of small and medium-sized churches whose pastors possess teaching skill with certain age levels should consider joining together — community by community — in some instances maintaining their several identities as congregations while establishing a single Protestant strategy for teaching. Thus the pastor of First Church of denomination X might specialize in teaching juniors of the associated Protestant churches; the pastor of Memorial Church of denomination Y, teaching the junior high age; and so on. Or, one man might major in teaching the Old Testament, another the New Testament, yet another church history.

At once the question arises, If interparish teaching is adopted, does the pastor-teacher relate to the families of his pupils in the same way as proposed under the single-parish plan? In other words, would a Presbyterian minister to Baptist families, a Baptist to Methodist families, and so forth? Given irenic pastors of the co-operating churches and a community in which all concerned subordinate denominational interests to Christian fellowship, each teacher-pastor can minister to the families of his pupils regardless of what particular churches they belong to. Idealistic? Certainly. And so is Christian faith, and the ecumenical church. Even now some communities enjoy genuine interparish unity. For instance, in a celebrated New England parish two churches of different denominations have a united program comprised of a single church school and a single every member canvass and budget, though each church has its own pastor and worship service. This is the kind of interparish situation in which the next advance might readily be made toward minister-taught classes. Already it is the practice of the two churches to consider the needs they have in common when a new pastor is to be called. In this situation it is especially important to choose a pastor partly on the basis of his teaching speciality. It happens that the present pastors of the united parish could teach the adolescents and possibly also the junior age pupils. Fortunately the public schools are only a step away from the parish house, and children frequently take part in choirs, clubs, and other afterschool events held there. Further, as in the case of numbers of churches, this parish places its facilities at the disposal of a weekday nursery unrelated to church teaching. A third professional is needed, therefore, either a man or a woman, skilled in teaching young children and in guiding the Christian growth of their families.

Mention of a woman minister brings up the question of her role in the church. On occasion I have been challenged, and rightly so, for intimating that the seminary-trained woman, because she is a woman, is more gifted with young children than with other ages; and for implying that only men are to serve as pastor-teachers of older pupils. Now certainly not sex but personal aptitude and interest determine what age levels either the male or the female minister is to serve. And yet primary and younger classes will generally have to be staffed with women (converted educational directors?), if for no other reason than that male pastors will probably remain in short supply for this ministry, even though nursery and kindergarten groups greatly need the male teacher. More precisely, they need both the male and female, working together, and when churches awaken to the value to be derived from thoroughly competent nursery and family guidance, young families will gain extraordinary spiritual help. Of the various approaches to inaugurating church education, this one may offer the richest returns.

In this connection, churches can profit by the kind of

work Everett S. Ostrovsky [26] has done with kindergarten children, although outside the church. His book records both the acute needs many young children in our society have for surrogate fathers to love them and heal them and enable them to learn, and the ability of a man to give children that which a woman teacher cannot do alone. The story of Dr. Ostrovsky's "secular" ministry to confused and deprived children, if applied to the work of pastor-teachers with young children and their families, would transform most of the churches' nursery and kindergarten programs. And churches would cease viewing these classes as responsibilities to be left to untrained women and immature girls on Sunday mornings, or to people oriented to partial goals who may simply use parish facilities for housing a weekday enterprise of limited scope.

This is not to say that seminary-trained men and women are to conduct classes for the very young without lay assistance; it is to stress the belief that every person in the church ought to understand that opportunities are going to waste for starting young families off right in Christian growth. The prevalence of broken homes denotes particular need of children for a father figure, a pastor. With training, empathy, and pastoral commitment the male teacher can render to young children one of the most-needed services within Protestantism. That he can seldom if ever engage in this work when he is a church's only minister is taken for granted, but because little children also need a pastor the churches are confronted with one more reason why they ought to consider very carefully the possibility of interparish education. Certainly, imaginative and bold new designs are in order if Protestants are to enjoy the fullness of Christian teaching and ministry. We shall have occasion to look further at the problem of personnel in the discussion of a curriculum for training professional ministers.

Much of the success parishes may have in shifting to church education hinges on overcoming an attitude that puts almost everything in the child's experience ahead of the church. For many families a second (weekend) home, like a second car, is becoming customary in our urbanized and suburbanized society; and some churches report greater success in getting students for weekday classes than for Sunday study and worship. Others seriously doubt their ability to take children away from school and community affairs for church education. We have already noted that we are confronted by a most difficult problem as we attempt to qualify youths' absorption in sports and other afterschool activities. One pastor and his colleague, an educational director who is also a mother of high school boys, took different positions on this issue, the mother contending that an appeal to her sons to give up just one weekday period for a church class would meet with no success. In fact, she went on to say, she is convinced that the boys need their athletic program *daily*. To this the pastor responded that daily organized sports carry a good thing too far. Moreover, he asserted, his colleague had lost sight of the importance of her sons' having substantial Christian teaching. The mother replied that they were enjoying rather good teaching in the Sunday school.

There are several points to be faced here, the first being the very evident one that even a professional worker may question the need for church education. Assuredly one ought to avoid being doctrinaire about the scheduling of classes, but usually Sunday morning is less conducive to serious study than a weekday. Furthermore, by holding church classes in the midst of regular weekly events, Christian faith is set closer to all of life's issues; hence, it may more readily call in question a large part of pupils' values and practices. At the very least, church teaching during the week fosters the understanding that religion is not something to be relegated to Sunday but is a quality of thinking and living that permeates ongoing experience. Rather than trying to *avoid* bringing forward the claims of the church on youth's time and interest, we should welcome the opportunity that the idea of church education entails for doing just that. Once the professional staff agrees that church education is needed as a means for elevating the quality of parish teaching and personal living, the education committee, official board, parents, and children will be consulted and invited to help set up a parish school of high standards.

In some cases church education will appeal more to laymen than to clergymen, or more to certain groups of pupils than to their parents. To be sure, the reaction from parish to parish will vary, but it remains true that a surprising number of lay people want their church to offer only competent teaching, if for no other reason than that they desire the best of everything. They see no reason why a local church cannot be a respectable educational enterprise. Indeed, these lay spokesmen are unimpressed by the few professionals who maintain that the church is at present doing a competent job of educating its communicants. And happily one hears of youth classes that gather on their own initiative for weekday instruction by a minister-teacher. For the past year and a half, so reports one such teacher, a high school group has met faithfully on Monday evenings, in attentive study of the Bible, particularly the eschatological passages. Several of the boys in the class are delinquents on probation. They dash up in their hot rods and, cigarette in mouth and Bible under arm, leap for the church steps. One may speculate that their teacher's Biblical and theological ministry, combined with his evident trust and love for his students, is keeping these delinquents out of prison. And if the whole story of this student-teacher relationship were known, it could likely be said that mutual affection has flowered into concern to know the truth about God with respect to human destiny. And surely Christian grace infuses the classroom as the teacher-theologian mediates divine love to youth whose personal histories prove that this sort of study is a novel experience for them.

Another high school group, composed of seniors, requested their pastor to conduct a Saturday morning class in ethics, thus preparing them for leaving home for college. A magnetic, vigorously masculine person with Christian integrity and scholarship, this pastor too elicits respect and desire for instruction. His parishioner-students are products of a privileged community and an excellent school system. Their willingness to study Christian ethics perhaps derives as much from desire to have a close and continuing relationship with their pastor as from their need to be fortified for the college world. The point to be underscored here is that both groups of students admire their teachers as persons and recognize that they know subject matter. In neither case has the teacher or the church he represents tried to force students to attend classes. Instead, teachers rely on establishing personal relations with the students and satisfying their religious interests. With older adolescents and adults this tactic is especially conducive to vital class participation, despite the fact that numerous events compete with the church for students' time and interest. And surely pupils of all ages will support church education when (a) they are drawn to the teacher, (b) they know he likes them, (c) he is a master of his subject, (d) he makes rigorous demands with respect to the learning task, and (e) the class enjoys one another and has a sense of accomplishment in meeting fundamental spiritual needs.

When people gather to examine proposals for establishing church education, invariably someone asks if there is a church anywhere in which the full program is in operation. Necessarily, I answer that so far as I know there is none. Yet the more people I see and the more who write, the greater is the number of churches found to have *aspects* of the program. This is heartening. It foreshadows the turn of a tide that can only eventuate in strengthening the growth of young and old in grace and knowledge of our Lord. And who can say what pause will come to parents and other members of a congregation when youth elect to meet their pastor for study that means limiting the ordinary round of events associated with adolescents? The fact is that parents of high school students particularly need the help of the pastor if unstable youth are to be guided into right living. And so do parents of exemplary youth, if old and young are to effect a proper balance between the many good things available to them and the most central thing, namely, their relationship to God and commitment to Christ.

We have looked at two competent church teachers, emphasizing that it is altogether possible to conduct classes during the week. And if classes, then why not a complete parish school? And if a school, why not a graduated curriculum [27] that includes evaluation of the student's progress and takes on something of the flavor of any good academic procedure? These are the features of a program to enlist students and cause them to view Christian growth as central in their lives.

This line of thought will not sound entirely strange to churches, for quite generally pastors have taught membership (confirmation) classes at stated weekday hours. Therefore, junior high students and their parents have come to expect at least this part of church education, indeed normally, to look forward to the experience. Two main incentives serve to gather a class of this sort: interest in uniting with the church (and in the process gaining clearer understanding of what is involved in Christian faith) and desire to form closer ties with the pastor. By capitalizing on pupils' expectancy in this regard, a pastor can rely on transfer of interest as he organizes other classes. This is no small impetus and it is to be taken into account as a parish considers the problem of establishing its school.

Further impetus for church education may derive from the custom in some communities of conducting released-time religious education, especially if oustanding work has been done. But where this program has been inferior both pupils and their parents may hesitate to try another kind of weekday teaching. In such situations, so far as possible released-time and church education are to be disassociated one from the other. After all, released-time religious education has been peripheral, viewed as supplementary to the Sunday school. But church education is central, comprehensive; it is the church, educating its communicants, and doing so with its best qualified personnel: pastor-teachers.

Yet another obstacle to church education is the viewpoint advanced by some contemporary spokesmen for

Christian nurture. Inasmuch as the church is the nurturing community, they reason that not only informal but also formal education is the task of the Christian fellowship as a whole. This I accept as sound, in so far as nurture largely takes place by influence: by the example of person related to person, by the more or less unconscious adoption of Christian attitudes derived from interpersonal relations, by family experiences avowedly Christian, and by participation in the worshiping community. But as indispensable as all these facets of nurture are, can it be said that they add up to comprehensive education in the historic faith and in informed Christian living? Those who answer affirmatively nevertheless do their very best to supplement teaching-by-influence with a somewhat more systematic and substantial teaching that they hope the Sunday school affords. This is the crux of the matter: the amateur Sunday school is not substantial enough. If you want your child to learn music, you find a teacher capable of imparting something more than appreciation of music. If you believe the young should grow up cherishing democratic values, you recognize that beyond living in a democratic ethos they require systematic and continuing teaching-learning experiences, which, in turn, require academic establishments staffed with the most fully informed teachers and practitioners of democracy available. No one questions society's decisive choice of academic halls to carry the main responsibility for education, nor is there any minimizing, under this system, of the crucial importance of the family and community as a whole in predisposing school children to take advantage of formal education. So be it with the teaching of the church.

Objections are sometimes raised to the effect that church teaching is necessarily different from the teaching process in general education, and that consequently the same rigorous teaching-learning standards do not apply to both undertakings. If this be true, then certainly let us be satisfied with the Sunday school and ignore any plea for making of the church a first-rate educational community. Which really is better, the Sunday school setting — in which goals are likely to be vague, preparation by pupils and teacher scant, measurement neglected, and a sense of progress dim — or an academic procedure very like that in a preparatory school where students respect the standards of the teacher of religion and give themselves to accomplishing the goals held before them?

Pastors are saying: " I really would like to teach in the church "; " I have long felt that something had to be done to improve our educational offering "; " Let me know if any of these peculiar opportunities cross your desk." And some are grasping the fact that they and their people can set to work right where they are and design church education. As one man expresses it, " This means I'll have to turn over much of the administrative work to laymen." Another wonders how he can cut down on the seven hours a week he spends at the telephone.

And there are requests and observations from the seminary. A student says: " Where can I learn to teach children? I wouldn't be interested in the limited work of a director of religious education, but church education definitely appeals to me." A professor says, " Does church education mean that all seminary students are expected to learn to teach, engaging in required teaching experiences as in required preaching courses? "

In answer to the last question I reply that I remain faithful to the New Testament principle of varieties of gifts, that I anticipate that only a minority — say not more than 40 per cent of seminarians — will soon undertake teaching as a part of their pastoral work, but that further I believe no greater percentage of B.D. candidates should be excused from trying to learn to teach than may be excused from courses in preaching. For how does a student or a faculty know that a given individual may not come to value teaching, once he gets a taste of it by doing it and learns to view it as basic in pastoral ministry?

In this chapter I have sought to show that pastors can learn to teach and can find the time for it; the problem of professional personnel is soluble; church education is second to nothing in the child's life; and formal church teaching is needed to complement the contribution of the nurturing community. In the next chapter we shall go farther into the problem of personnel and deal with graduate school courses of study for preparing minister-teachers.

7

Recruitment and Preparation

Local church leaders seeking to transmute the Sunday school into a comprehensive program of church education may be asked (as I have been on occasion), "Why not go the whole way and substitute a parochial school for the public school?" A small number of Protestants have moved in this direction, but it is a move far from necessary or desirable. It is unnecessary because a system that relates pastor and pupils for formal learning, and pastor and the families of the pupils for close and continuing guidance, offers greater promise than do parochial schools for helping persons to develop within the Christian fellowship. It is undesirable for several reasons, one of them being that not simply a school's services but also an improved pastoral ministry is the aim of church education. Therefore, the parochial school hardly suffices. Moreover, if Protestants in large numbers were to forsake the public schools, they would weaken them and hence diminish the American ideal of democratic education by means of which a pluralistic society is nourished and unified.

Most of the contemporary interest in the teaching of religion bypasses the parochial issue and envisions some kind of alliance between religionists and educators. Since the Second World War extensive study has been given to the relation of religion to public education, notably by Dr. F. Ernest Johnson and his associates on the American Council on Education, by groups within the National Education Association, by the Religious Education Association, and by the National Council of the Churches of Christ in the U.S.A. I am sympathetic with the belief that tax-supported schools have an *educational* responsibility for teaching about the great religions. And certainly an exponent of church education is in agreement with the conviction that though public education might one day give a fairly good grounding in knowledge of Christianity, the churches would still have to teach in order for pupils to know Christ and commit themselves to him. The point to be stressed here is that although those who are concerned with education in religion, and religion in education, realize in part that the church is ultimately responsible for persons learning of Christ, they have neglected to devise a system more adequate than that of the so-called church school. Subsumed under "church school," of course, is the Sunday school, the vacation church school, weekday released-time classes, youth and adult groups, and more. In contrast, what church education signifies is less the establishment of another school than the educational fulfillment of the church. In other words, church education *is* the church, engaged in teaching — teaching so far as possible carried on by pastors, their work supplemented by lay ministers.

This brings us to consideration of teaching personnel from a somewhat different angle from any yet discussed in these pages, namely, the recruitment and academic preparation of minister-teachers, ordained or not. Where are candidates to be found? Even if the two-hundred-thousand-odd Protestant pastors [28] having charges were competent and wished to do so, they could not handle the thirty-seven and a quarter million pupils enrolled in the Sunday schools. Teaching on this scale would involve at least twice as many minister-teachers as the number of pastors now active. (Admittedly, constantly changing figures, to say nothing of averages, have little bearing on a given local situation.) And in the light of the continuing difficulty of securing enough schoolteachers, nurses, social workers, and other humanitarian professionals, wherein might the churches hope for a sufficient number of minister-teachers? To draw the picture yet more unfavorably we need only remind ourselves of the fact that clergymen's salaries are low; they have not kept pace with the cost of living.

A recent study of 2,201 ministers of nine different denominations comprising a membership of almost twenty-three million [29] indicates that the average cash salary of all respondents was $4,436, a figure somewhat improved when parsonage and other allowances are taken into consideration. As a whole, the study substantiates the impression that the smaller churches in rural communities and small towns often fail to pay enough to support a pastor and his family. Quite commonly the pastor's expenses — particularly for his automobile — further impoverish him. More hopeful are the authors' findings that churches of one thousand or more members provide a total average compensation of almost $8,000; churches with multiple staffs provide an average salary of about $9,550 for the senior pastor, " as against $5,580 for subordinates "; and that more than " 85 per cent of the ministers in the sample serving churches with 1,000 or more members are members of . . . multiple staffs." [30]

It would seem that as the population continues to grow a considerable proportion of the churches will employ multiple staffs. Meanwhile, the cry is for educational directors, and frequently their remuneration exceeds the average salaries of pastors. Young men and women need not think that as minister-teachers they would go hungry, for as laymen visualize the significance of church education, suitable salaries will be forthcoming, certainly in the larger churches and in united parish programs of the smaller churches. We may foresee, then, greater incentive to greater numbers of college youth to enter graduate study leading toward the professional ministry. But — pursuing the recruitment problem on the assumption that Protestants will need about another 200,000 ministers, and this based on the *present* church enrollment — it is apparent that a source of supply other than the present college generation must be found. There are several potential sources of supply.

Consider first the numbers of men who move back and forth between the pastorate and denominational and interdenominational executive positions of many kinds. True, some find satisfaction in desk work and travel and stay with it, but perhaps there are hundreds more who — though not quite at home in typical pastoral responsibilities — long for the close pastoral ties envisioned in this volume. The remoteness of secretarial ministers from the development of persons heightens for many their desire to be shepherds of a flock. Not only so, when churches do make provision for pastoral teaching, there will be less need for denominational education boards and publishing houses to continue their manifold efforts to direct unskilled lay teaching. How many thousands of prospective minister-teachers might thus be released to local churches (and how much money could thereby be reallocated to support church education), is something to cause wonder.

Now lest employees of area and national staffs feel that these observations are intended as an attack on them, I assure them that I am but calling into question the *system* within which they operate, for it is inseparable from the teaching and pastoral system under which local churches now operate. And this must be changed at whatever price. Doubtlessly many laymen can join me in thinking immediately of certain field secretaries, denominational publicists, and others whom they would like to see in local churches, serving as minister-teachers. And very likely the majority of those who might make this shift would experience fulfillment — personal and spiritual — more readily than in the vast machinery of continent-wide, impersonal endeavor now draining them.

Next, there are married women and retired men, both seminary trained, who could be enlisted to serve the churches in a professional capacity. Many of them would require refresher courses and assistance in adapting themselves to the pastor-teacher idea, but this need not constitute an insurmountable difficulty. At present hundreds — possibly thousands — of women who have earned a seminary or school of religious education degree, not only feel that they owe it to the church and themselves to use their educational preparation but would be able to do so if they were given suitable opportunity. As wives and mothers these women are probably less inclined to engage in the endless managerial work of directors of religious education than in a limited program of classroom teaching and pastoral relations with assigned groups of families.

Another source of supply comes to mind. Churches and seminaries bent on educating minister-teachers would be enlightened by reading the lists of faculties published in college catalogues. Numbers of professors in disciplines other than religion hold the B.D. and similar advanced degrees. Couple this fact with the growing trend toward retired academics' entering upon other work, and possibilities are seen for the churches' recruiting their services. As I write, a letter comes to hand from a man, with but one year to go as a university professor, who, after seminary, spent the first thirty years of his professional life with the church in missionary and educational enterprises. In his words, he now wishes to "bring together the first years of . . . life with the last; the first years with the church and the last with public education." He goes on to speak of doing this as a free lance, yet any local church would be fortunate to have this particular man as a pastor-teacher, for he is resourceful and versatile. Only in years do men like him age, and many remain productive far beyond the age of retirement. One can but covet the broad and incisive leadership they might give churches ready to make teaching equal to the best in general education. Imagination is quickened by the prospect of bringing on the American scene an inclusive education wherein church teaching — kept distinct and free from entanglements with the state — becomes integral to the whole of the child's intellectual and spiritual development.

And then there are the laymen who could be prepared for the role of the minister-teacher. A minister writes: "I am persuaded that there are capable lay people, men and women, in many of our churches who, though they do not have a seminary degree, could be given special training, perhaps at our seminaries, and who could bring to the [teaching] task devotion and skill beyond that of a great many ministers." Exactly — or, almost exactly.

Let us suppose that a local church has two or three lay members who definitely possess gifts, desire, and time for serving as teachers of the young and as pastors to their families. Shall these prospective lay ministers be invited to go to work at once, or is there a better policy to follow? It will be helpful to take a cue from public education. In the better school systems every effort is made to abide by agreed-upon standards for employing teachers, and despite the fact that inflexible regulations occasionally deprive children of a superior teacher — because of some deficiency in the candidate's academic record — for the most part schools are safeguarded by boards of accreditation.[31] At times temporary or emergency certificates are issued, but, when possible, prospective teachers are required to return to college in order to ensure their preparation for classroom work. Perhaps to a greater extent than may at first seem feasible, prospective church teachers could study in a theological school, or at least in a school of religious education, before undertaking to serve as minister-teachers.

Notwithstanding the value of learning to teach on the job — under a fully trained and competent pastor-teacher — laymen, though expecting to remain outside the ranks of the ordained clergy, ought to have full ministerial training; or, as a second best, partial training by means of a two-year seminary or school or religious education curriculum leading toward a master's degree in education. Seldom or never should churches call persons any less qualified. However, an exception might be made of highly capable men and women who, though without a college degree and therefore ineligible for an advanced degree, successfully carry seminary or school of religious education courses. Actually the American Association of Theological Schools allows its member schools to admit a limited number of degreeless students; and indeed it sometimes happens that a special student has superior intelligence and aptitude for the ministry. In increasing numbers, such people might well be recruited by the churches and encouraged to enter seminaries, not only with the blessing of the church but also with its financial backing.

There are, then, remarkable sources of supply besides the college generation for staffing the churches with minister-teachers, among them being denominational executives and publicists, wives and retired men who hold a divinity degree, and selected laymen. Because particular attention should be given to a curriculum for training laymen — whose formal study would probably seldom extend to the full three- or four-year B.D. curriculum — we shall examine a two-year program of studies suitable both to schools of religious education and to seminaries.

Not all laymen will be interested in the remainder of this chapter (for it mainly concerns theological educators), but anyone considering preparing himself to serve the church may read with profit. And, it is hoped, laymen who are members of boards of directors of schools of religious education and seminaries will be edified.

◇

It is instructive to note that the school of religious education has sought to be to the churches what the teachers college is to the public schools. Both have weighted their curriculums on the side of tool or professional courses, which in some instances appear out of balance with foundational or content courses. As a reaction against knowledge for knowledge's sake, and instruction often uninteresting and ineffectual, quite understandably programs of study in secular and religious education sometimes swing to extreme functionalism. But with the revival of theology, church educators are looking for graduate curriculums more appropriate for preparing professional leaders to accentuate the renewal of the church as the nurturing community. What principles and objectives are desirable?

I wish to make three proposals directed to those who design graduate curriculums and to laymen wishing to become minister-teachers. Also, I shall suggest the kind of study that might engage future church administrators.

The first proposal is that the curricular gap between schools of religious education and seminaries be closed and that the relationship of laymen to ordained ministers be thoroughly understood. Just as the teachers college nowadays takes on certain aspects of the liberal arts college, so the school of religious education may well reflect more of the character and curriculum of the seminary. True, the school of religious education has evolved for the purpose of training lay workers (who unfortunately tend to view themselves as something less than ministers), and its mission has generally been conceived of differently from that of the theological seminary. Nevertheless, in any school, courses of study aimed at preparing church leaders ought to be duly weighted with theological disciplines. This is hardly the situation today. On the other hand, current concern with making the gospel relevant, communication of the faith, the use of dialogue in theological discourse, and the need to develop the mutual ministry of laymen and clergymen all point directly to the necessity for seminarians' becoming educationally competent. Therefore, curriculums of the school of religious education and the seminary ought to permeate each other, for graduates of both types of institutions are ready to serve the church better if they have followed studies in which education and theology are integrated. Thus the educator may become a practical theologian while the theologian becomes an educator.

Be it recalled that professional leaders who are thoroughly grounded in the Christian heritage and the educational process regard the church as the redemptive, nurturing community. Moreover, their relationships with one another reflect oneness of spirit and purpose. It may be said quite plainly that where misunderstanding or rivalry has caused a breach between the educational and pastoral ministries, the chances are that the educator and the pastor have come to their work from programs of study that failed to unify education and theology, teaching and preaching, administration and pastoral care. Certainly there is reason for distress when a church educator ignores the historic and Biblical dimensions of Christian faith, or when a pastor minimizes the teaching function of the church. Parenthetically, let it be admitted that sometimes not misunderstanding or ignorance but valid judgment leads either the educator or the pastor to criticize adversely the work of the other. Indeed, approval should be withheld from educational programs that deal with superficial moralisms to the exclusion of theological depth, just as approval is to be denied pastoral efforts aimed at statistical triumphs to the neglect of the congregation's growth in grace.

With churches becoming larger, their ministries more specialized, and professional staffs having to learn how to operate harmoniously and efficiently, bigness and complexity are aggravated by compartmentalization. And when energy is consumed by organizational requirements the meaning and life of the fellowship as Christian community is vitiated. Leaders and the led, therefore, often find themselves trapped in an intricate operation, not with organism but with organization dominant. They lose sight of their mission and of themselves as Christian persons. The question must be raised repeatedly, by the ordained and unordained: Who are we, under God? To answer this it is necessary to amplify what was said in the previous chapter.

When the idea is taken seriously that all men are called of God to be his ministers, serving one another and the world, a decisive move is made toward the view that there really is no essential difference between the ordained and the unordained. But if there is no difference in essence, in practice there is — one that is taken into account by the *fact* of ordination. And whatever else this rite means, it signifies special opportunity for the ordained to exercise particular gifts in serving the church. Furthermore, the pastor is expected to possess special knowledge of God — by virtue of having a seminary education and being privileged to keep studying while giving himself wholly to a life of devotion and parish work. Withal, his people count on his having a portion of grace that endows him with godliness. For how can he be *parson* — *the* person — unless his life and thought are imbued with the mind of Christ? To be sure, if he looks upon himself as *the person,* he isn't what he thinks he is. But if he is a true parson, then he is seen by his people as a man full of truth and power.

The reader will bear in mind that we are focusing just now on the existing ministries of the church — not the one called for by church education — therefore it is necessary to appraise the status of the director of religious education and understand the breach too often apparent between the pastor and the educator.

The director, as a baptized Christian, should understand that he is a member of the priesthood of all believers, like all Christians called to be a minister within the communion of mutual ministers. In practice, and in the implicit view of many congregations, the director stands somewhere between the clergy and the laity, in most instances being closer to the latter. Even if ordained, he probably remains more on the side of the laity, particularly if he took his training in a school of religious education rather than in a seminary.

Certain related issues need to be faced at this point. Should the educational director sit among the prophets? — which is to say, among pastors instead of among the people. If a church insists on continuing the office of director, should the educator be as well prepared as the pastor in the several theological disciplines? In order to close the distance between pastors and educators, between preaching and teaching, between Christian fellowship and institutionalism, between redemptive interrelations and administrative proficiency, the chief servants — the pastor and the director — ought to be of one mind. If they are, each of them is more pastoral than promotional in his particular phase of the ministry; each possesses vision and competency best ensured by a graduate school in which theology and education are integrated in the curiculum.

◆

Inasmuch as the purposes of the church and its educational program are the same, " the increase of the love of God and neighbor," the second proposal is that curriculums in schools of religious education be designed — as in seminaries — for preparing men and women to make a distinctively pastoral approach to their service of the church. This does not mean that the two-year curriculum leading to the master's degree for educators, administrators, musicians, and the like need be abandoned, or that all schools of religious education ought to turn themselves into seminaries. However, if there is merit in the idea that teaching the gospel deserves as much preparation as preaching the gospel, and if the three-year B.D. curriculum is soundly based, there is much to be said for B.D. programs that are ready to offer courses and intern experience in teaching. Accordingly, some schools of religious education may well consider providing a B.D. curriculum, with a major in education, as an alternative to the M.R.E. curriculum. This they can perhaps do best in conjunction with neighboring seminaries.

Within the B.D. program of schools of religious education and seminaries alike specialized courses in teaching or administration or church music need not encroach on the larger part of the curriculum having to do with traditional theological disciplines and the work of pastoral care. A student headed for a ministry other than that of preaching should be able to substitute education courses for all or most work in homiletics. And the prospective pastor — who plans to be primarily a preacher and parish leader — needs to understand the nurture process and learn to teach, for reasons I shall mention presently. Thus his course of study should include work in education.

Eventually the curriculums of schools of religious education and seminaries may well become more similar than dissimilar; hence, students looking toward filling church positions as teachers, preachers, and administrators will readily attend the same schools, studying together in many or most of the same classes, thereby *together* learning to see the whole task of Christian leadership. This would mean that in the future the larger churches could expect greater staff harmony and unity of purpose; and the very large church might have a collegiate ministry that would provide a pastor for each section of the whole flock. To reiterate, the principle of varieties of gifts and of varieties of service would still prevail, but within the structure of the collegium each pastor would fulfill his ministerial office largely by formal teaching of children and youth, informal teaching of adults, and guidance of the families he is called to serve. Let it be underscored that all members of the collegium need not be ordained, yet all are to be ministers — some, pastors to designated groups of families; some, servants at large, such as the administrator, the musician, the parish visitor. The senior pastor will have the B.D. degree or its equivalent; others, at least the M.R.E. degree or its equivalent. Each will employ his aptitudes and gifts as pastor, teacher, preacher, though the head pastor will do most or all of the preaching while a colleague will be the principal teacher. In the smaller church, accustomed to a pastor and an educational director, there will be the same two leaders known henceforth simply as pastors — one, designated preacher, the other, perhaps, designated teacher — and both may do some preaching and teaching. Responsibility for administration and pastoral care will be divided according to their particular abilities.

Obviously this is another argument that favors elevating the status of church educators and requires of them a distinctive professional preparation, while requiring future preachers to learn how to teach. Here we must be very careful, for already curriculums and church tasks are taxing on one's time and energy.

It is just at this point that the present school of religious education and perhaps its less academically gifted students seem most suited to meet a major need, that of church administration. Doubtlessly religious educators are the first persons to admit that that administration is best which is educationally rooted, and that the curriculums of schools of religious education are better conceived for teaching administrative leadership than are those of most seminaries. Not only so, in view of pastors' recognized dislike for administration, coupled with the fact that many of them are forced to spend the major part of their time at it, denominational boards and local churches would be wise to look to the school of religious education to supply administrators — laymen with the master's degree, devoted to the church, and possessing ability in church finance and program development. Such laymen, unlike many pastors, generally have the temperament, interest, and skill needed for administering the church. They are the doers, the activists, whereas the shepherd at his best is one who ponders, studies, preaches, teaches, and gives himself to persons at a truly pastoral level. Certainly more churches need to relieve the pastor of managerial details, conserving his talent and time for his particular office. He will remain the leader of the flock, but in order to do so he need not administer personally the manifold activities of the modern church; rather, the administrator — a lay minister of parish life — will assume this responsibility in far more churches than is now the case and enlist a corps of helpers.

But here again, just as the prospective church educator and prospective preacher need to study in the same school, and in many of the same courses, so the administrator-in-training needs to join them if a common outlook and unity of purpose are to characterize pastors and lay administrators. In a sense the two-year master's program leading toward church administration would be an abbreviated B.D. program, with several of the courses of the two curriculums being the same. And because a course of study is only a part of any school's curriculum, students intending to be administrators and those intending to become pastors, when on the same campus and participating together in the larger life of the school, would be partaking of the same atmosphere of learning and Christian living.

Granted that these proposals may be unacceptable to many, and that most schools of religious education and seminaries will prefer to remain as they are, it is significant that certain teachers colleges are becoming general colleges and liberal arts colleges are unifying their arts and science courses with practical work in training professional educators.

The third proposal deals more specifically with a two-year graduate course of study for prospective church teachers and administrators. The list of basic courses below conforms to the stipulation of the American Association of Schools of Religious Education of thirty semester hours in foundational study, ten courses; and eighteen semester hours in practical work, for which six professional courses may be the equivalent — plus intern requirements — leading toward the M.R.E. degree.[32] But unlike the student following the customary M.R.E. program, under the plan outlined here a student may receive the degree by earning as few as forty-eight semester-hour credits and by demonstrating professional competency. A semester load is not to exceed five courses; hence, the student is to do his work more thoroughly than is possible when he carries six or eight courses a semester.

BASIC COURSES

(Exceptions allowed according to the student's past experience and needs)

FIRST YEAR

First Semester

Old Testament
New Testament
Church History
Social Ethics (Church and Community)
The Nurture Process (Principles of teaching-learning, conducted in connection with observation or practice teaching in a demonstration class of the School of Religious Education, or in some other suitable classroom situation. This course may be delayed until the second semester, if practice teaching is to begin then. In this event Christian Worship is taken during the first semester. Students majoring in Administration may substitute a course in church polity.)

Second Semester

Teaching the Bible
History of Christian Doctrine
    or
History of Education (With particular attention to church and state relations)
Church School Curriculums (Majors in Administration may substitute a course in church management)
Christian Worship (Church music and forms of worship for various age levels)

SECOND YEAR

First Semester

Teaching the Bible

Theology

Leadership Skills (Guidance of individuals and groups; lay leadership education)

Seminar for Teachers (I) (Concurrent with intern teaching. Age-level characteristics; lesson planning and evaluation; the use of drama, arts, and crafts)

or

Seminar for Administrators (I) (In connection with intern experience in a church or a related institution. Church architecture, building codes, legal issues)

Second Semester

Missions, or World Religions, or The Ecumenical Church

Educational Leadership (Organization and human relations in administration and supervision)

Seminar for Teachers (II)

or

Seminar for Administrators (II)

A paragraph is in order concerning the foundational courses. Bible courses are conceived of as a study of the record of God's mighty acts among the people of the Old and New Covenant, his disclosure of himself and his redemptive work through his Son, the Word of truth made flesh. The course in Church History presents the story of the life of the church, viewed as the body of Christ in which the Holy Spirit dwells and imbues the persons in the fellowship of forgiveness. Social Ethics explores tensions existing where the church meets the world in the events of the community, and shows wherein the Christian ethic illuminates or resolves these tensions. The History of Christian Doctrine and the course on systematic theology acquaint the student with human effort to refine the meaning of God in relation to man and history. The History of Education — a suggested alternate for the History of Christian Doctrine — includes attention to the American educational scene, particularly with respect to the problem of church and state and the teaching of religion. The study of Christian worship is designed to explicate the holy and corporate act of the worshiping community so that by the sung and spoken word children, youth, and adults may be led to praise God. Courses on the world mission of the church, the great religions, and the ecumenical church seek to enlarge the student's knowledge and enable him to see wherein his denomination fits into the whole religious picture.

It will be noted that courses on teaching the Bible are excluded for the moment from foundational subjects. We turn now to professional courses.

The first of these, The Nurture Process, combines theories of teaching and learning with practice — practice desirably involving at least two age levels as a means for helping the student find his special competence. The second course, Church School Curriculums, makes an analysis and comparison of selected church school curriculums and stimulates the student to construct a curriculum suitable for the kind of local church in which he may teach upon graduation. The third professional course, Leadership Skills, experiments with leadership skills, introduces ways to guide individuals and groups, and presents the issues of dynamic lay leadership education to be carried on in the local church. The fourth provision for professional training embraces seminars for teachers held concurrently with intern experiences. These together focus on pupils' developmental stages and deal with appropriate methods of handling subject matter in a variety of ways. Data on pupils' actual classroom experiences — written up by the student teacher, or his teaching partner alternating with him as an observer — are brought to the seminar and used as a medium of instruction.

Both seminars for teachers and courses on teaching the Bible — the latter reflecting a combination of elements of content and professional courses — constitute occasions for wrestling with the twofold problem of selecting and teaching the Biblical materials according to pupils' capacity. Students are encouraged to devise their own courses for use when they shall have entered upon their careers, for surely the professional church teacher of the future will be no more inclined than the college and preparatory school teacher of religion to rely on present Sunday school curricular materials. We shall return to this issue in Chapter 9.

It may be remarked in passing that good Bible teaching generally takes place in colleges and preparatory schools rather than in the churches. This situation will have to be corrected by the school of religious education and the seminary. To this end it will be remembered that story and play, drawing and painting, are suitable for introducing elementary age children to the Bible and related subjects. These teaching media, plus drama, choric speech, audio-visual aids, and elementary research may be used with older children. With adolescents interlocutory teaching — teaching as dialogue and prompting — may follow upon the use of pupil assignment of reading and reports to the class. These and other methods occupy student teachers in seminars as they evaluate their teaching of pupils.

Seminars for administrators give large place to church architecture, its Christian symbolism as well as its functionalism, its art forms as well as its appropriateness to a given congregation at worship, at study, and at work. Be it noted that the seminars are preceded by a course in church polity, which the prospective administrator ordinarily takes instead of The Nurture Process, and by a course in church management as a substitute for Church School Curriculums. However, in some instances the future administrator and teacher each will elect courses in the field of the other, partly in recognition of the fact that students often do not know what professional tasks will engage them until they are actually on the job and partly because any student may profit by familiarity with both disciplines.

The course entitled Educational Leadership very definitely brings future administrators and teachers together. Presently at Andover Newton this course uses the case method to simulate professional leaders' handling of church situations.

Laymen may be thinking that the pros and cons of a specific graduate curriculum raise forbidding issues; yet, there is a good deal to be said for their gaining some conception of the kind of study that might engage those considering serving the church professionally. It should be made perfectly clear that the curriculum just proposed conceives of ministries that, for the most part, are yet to be inaugurated, and presumes to lead churches in a manner consistent with the views expressed throughout this volume. Will such a curriculum be widely adopted? And will Protestants move toward church education?

Whether hopeful or doubtful about eventual adoption

of church education, it will prove practical for all who see a measure of promise in the minister-teacher idea to proceed without delay by making full use of existing course offerings in accredited schools of religious education and seminaries. These institutions — led respectively by the American Association of Schools of Religious Education and the American Association of Theological Schools (one could wish that they might merge) — are constantly addressing themselves to improving their curriculums. Perhaps they will be constrained to reckon with the churches' need for pastor-teachers. And because it seems that something of a trend is emerging toward seminary-sponsored, short-term courses and institutes for laymen, the idea of church education may give point and purpose to these offerings.

It is fairly common for laymen in late youth or middle age to leave their occupations and enter schools of religious education or seminaries with the expectation of serving the church in a professional capacity. In many instances they are unclear as to what phase of the professional ministry they are suited for. For them the two-year curriculum is often a proper vehicle during a period of transition. However, with the sharpening of focus and discovery that advanced study is within their capacity, some of these students quite properly shift to a full course of theological study.

In sum, let it be said that both schools of religious education and seminaries are invited to undertake to train men and women for the work of pastor-teacher, and for allied ministries. While a two-year master's program of studies is helpful, a more extensive one, leading toward the B.D. degree, is preferable. But the latter requires new formulation and to this task we turn next.

8

Memorandum to Seminaries and Supporters

MORE INCLUSIVE and more to be desired than the two-year curriculum described in the previous chapter is the B.D. degree program capped by exacting intern training. This latter directly concerns local churches, for it is to them that seminaries must look not only to serve as a base for intern training but also to help subsidize students. And because this kind of education is more expensive than ordinary theological study, the seminary has to enlist generous contributors including philanthropic foundations and business corporations interested in thoroughgoing improvement of the Protestant ministry. And if there are insufficient funds to subsidize all its students, the seminary may devise a more limited plan by an affiliation with a few strong churches in its vicinity. In any case, intern training requires a working agreement between seminaries and local churches.

If duly strengthened, field work (more properly called in-service training) might evolve into an internship plan. Generally speaking, first year B.D. candidates should serve in churches only as laymen and unpaid volunteers, conserving their time for study. It is especially important that students entering seminary straight from college shall work unremittingly at their books, for many of them have had little background in Biblical faith or in liberal arts. And if the student's usual need for remunerative employment does yield to his educational need, this places a heavy load on scholarship funds because, alas, ministerial candidates are seldom self-supporting. On the other hand, though he seems unable to realize it, the junior student who does not take employment as a field worker — and certainly not in a distant church — can do without an automobile. Actually, seminary administrators would be well advised to investigate the extent to which students suppose they simply *must* have a car, in order to engage in field work; must have field work in order to support the car — plus, like as not, having additional subsidy from the seminary to complete the job of supporting the car.

By limiting church participation during first-year seminary study, it is less likely that the student will be cast prematurely in the role of a professional leader; or be too early subjected to the risk of forming distaste for church work, due to trying to carry responsibilities beyond his capacity. The second year, then, ordinarily becomes the student's initial experience in remunerative field work. Graduated to the student's ability, field work contributes to his learning to be a minister. However necessary the earning of money may be, it is widely recognized by seminaries and supporting churches that the student's development is primary. This first semiprofessional venture can acquaint him with what is involved in conducting at least a *phase* of the work of the church; for example, assisting with a youth group, or making pastoral calls. Assuming the church is collaborating with the seminary in effecting a transition from Sunday school to church education and can subsidize a small group of seminarians for three years each, the middler launches out on a relatively long-term experience aimed at training him as pastor, preacher, and teacher. He has tutorial conferences with the head pastor — or another designated member of the church staff — and director of field work, and discharges assigned tasks under their supervision. Classroom teaching, full responsibility for leading youth groups and preaching usually are left to the second year or to the third, when he becomes an intern. In instances of churches' furnishing the whole of students' stipends, enlightened laymen and pastors will view first-year in-service training as their contribution to theological education, therefore, expect only the exceptional student to earn his keep until later.

In the senior year, normally the student will remain in the same church and undertake greater responsibilities. Thus he may become the leader of a youth group with which he worked previously as an assistant leader. During the fall semester he is apprenticed to a pastor-teacher on a practice-teaching basis and by spring he may be ready to teach. As time permits he attends selected board meetings, by way of introduction to the larger task of ministerial leadership, and engages in other duties for which the tutor-pastor thinks he is ready. But he is still a student, a learner whose time on the church job must be balanced with a full academic load. Consequently, the church will help him limit his hours on the job to twelve to fifteen a week, including preparation. Conversely, if the situation demands, the church and the seminary together will see to it that the field worker observes the hours for which he has contracted.

Thus we have before us a sketch of two years of supervised, remunerative church work, the second of which injects new elements into in-service training and somewhat changes its form as customarily practiced by seminaries.

Indeed, advanced field work might just as well be called the beginning of internship, for, when possible, it should be linked with the intern year — a year that under some plans now in operation is conducted after completion of senior year.

Interns are to be considered full-time members of the church staff, save for occasional seminars back at the seminary designed to aid them in their tasks as pastors, preachers, and teachers. As will be seen presently, this training integrates professional practice and seminar study. And when interns are serving in churches where they have had preliminary field work, they and the church stand to gain by virtue of common past experiences. It is the policy of one large church affiliated with a seminary in the East to take two new students a year, advancing them for a total of three years, the last one being the intern year. This means six seminarians a year working in the church, learning to be pastoral leaders and teachers. Clear distinction is made between a man's first two years — in-service training — and the final year — intern training — when he is working as one of the pastors of the church and engaging in all phases of professional leadership. The stipend for the first year takes care of seminary tuition, is raised during the second year, and for the intern year approximates the salary of a beginning pastor of the average church. While the argument is sometimes advanced that by remaining in the same church for three years of practical training a man denies himself opportunity to broaden his experience, it is probably more true to say that a single strong church — in which practice under guidance inducts the learner into the complexities of pastoral leadership — ensures the maximum in ministerial training. Furthermore, the church mentioned here offers the very experiences essential for preparing men and women to be the kind of pastors for which this book is calling. Let there be more churches like it working with seminaries!

It should be noted that there are few pastoral intern programs now in effect over the country, and that most of them place the intern experience between the middler and senior years. There are at least two serious drawbacks to this plan: the intern year is almost always spent in a new situation, unrelated to field work; and seldom if ever is it possible for the student to engage in concurrent seminary courses or have adequate guidance. Not so with the plan outlined here, for it gives both the supporting church and the student continuity impossible on a one-year intern basis; and it unifies foundational and professional courses with practical church tasks. In other words, it allows the student to remain in one place long enough to contribute to the life of the church, to gain assurance that he is ready to be a pastor, and to integrate theological disciplines with church leadership. The whole process enables the student to test himself and to know that he is fully tested. If he meets the requirements, he can be more highly commended to the church calling him than is ordinarily the case with a beginning pastor. Also, as will appear presently in items suggested for inclusion in intern training, the student benefits from what amounts to a year of advanced study beyond the B.D. degree. He should receive the B.D. upon completion of three years of study and the Th.M. at the end of the intern year. Furthermore, serious consideration might well be given by a seminary, in conjunction with the American Association of Theological Schools, to awarding the Doctor of Divinity degree (to intern-trained men and women), say, at the end of five years of outstanding pastoral leadership and the writing of an acceptable thesis. The advantages of making the D.D. an earned degree can be readily enumerated by anyone responsible for selecting people for honorary degrees.

◆

We now look more closely at the problem of relating professional courses to in-service and intern training, starting with the middler year and ending with the fourth or intern year. It is to be kept in mind that, given a suitable church in which to learn and work, the student remains in the same place for three years. In addition to regular foundational work in Bible, church history, theology, and the like, the B.D. candidate headed for the pastorate needs at least six professional courses taken during the middler and senior years — plus intensive seminars held throughout the intern year. In the fall of the middler year, when he begins supervised field work, he takes Pastoral Leadership (identical with Educational Leadership listed under the M.R.E. curriculum), The Conduct of Public Worship, and possibly an elective in Group Work or The Psychology of Personality. Second semester courses are Homiletics, Pastoral Care, and perhaps an elective in work with children, youth, and adults. In the first semester of the senior year the required course is The Nurture Process — which stresses principles of teaching-learning and fits in with the student's apprenticeship teaching in the affiliated church. A recommended elective is the Sociology of Church and Community. In the second semester the student takes either advanced preaching — in which attention is given to the preparation and delivery of sermons — or a course in Church Administration. The recommended elective is a Seminar for Teachers emphasizing age-level characteristics, lesson planning and evaluation, the use of drama, arts and crafts. Additional senior-year electives in professional courses are not encouraged because the student needs to reserve as much time as possible for thorough work in the traditional theological disciplines.

Now if a seminary can handle field work and related courses under its present administrative and teaching staff, the same can hardly be said for intern training. Even presupposing careful supervision on the part of affiliated churches, the seminary will very likely need one additional faculty member for each group of six to ten interns. Hence it is necessary to seek a sizable grant from philanthropic and business enterprises if intern training is to be required of all seminarians who expect to become pastors. The intern year must be seen for what it is: a highly intensive undertaking, *necessary* for training men to be pastors, preachers, and teachers. Just how intensive it is may be conveyed by the following stipulations.

The intern assists in the conduct of weekly adult or youth worship services; occasionally preaches; assumes administrative responsibility under guidance of the head pastor; carries six to eight hours of classroom teaching and familiarizes himself with his pupils in home, school, and community; ministers to individuals and their families; and gains some knowledge of the work of the wider church fellowship. He is accountable to his assigned tutor-pastor and to his seminary adviser, besides having to carry a full ministerial load and prepare for biweekly seminars at the seminary. In the seminars he spends a full day and evening with fellow students and instructors, analyzing the actual work he is doing in the church. Seminars require detailed reports: copies of worship services and sermons, lesson plans, verbatim accounts of pastoral care given in home and church, and more, all subjected to critical appraisal and supplementing the adviser's and the

tutor-pastor's observation of the intern on the job. Moreover, at least one session during the day back at the seminary involves some chosen academic exercise specifically
related to the interns' continuing intellectual and spiritual
growth. In sum, every effort is made to ensure both professional proficiency and personal development in the life
of faith, with an eye to genuine integration of works and
Christian belief.

Quite obviously some students cannot measure up to the
rigors of such a year, but those who do can be counted on
to become good pastors. More helpfully than in any other
way, perhaps, intern training enables the seminary and the
student to determine whether a man should lead a single-
pastor church, or serve as a member of a collegiate pastorate, or abandon the pastorate.

Since I have seen something of the demands on interns
and the seminary, the fact should not be obscured that
exacting requirements are also placed upon the affiliated
church. And although the life of a church may be enriched
by the training of field workers and interns, this is neither
the churches' primary religious or financial responsibility.
Only as their basic needs for Christian community are met
can they justifiably expend the tutorial hours and money
necessary to support intern training. A seminary striving
to develop a complement of churches affiliated for intern
training is fortunate if, in its vicinity, it finds a dozen that
are competent and willing. Aside from the financial subsidy involved a yet more important requirement is that
there shall be sympathetic laymen, and pastors exceptional enough to be both good practitioners and tutors.
High requirements indeed! And the seminary that sets out
to establish a valid internship program must be prepared
for a struggle. Some churches with money to spare for the

program cannot meet other standards. Other churches, with no money, may prove to be exactly the ones with which the seminary should affiliate. And this requires funds from the seminary.

Let us suppose that a small-scale beginning demonstrates the merit of interning. After a period of three to five years the seminary might require this work of all future pastors, or continue it as an elective open also to students of neighboring seminaries. Whatever the decision, a pioneering seminary is to have as its mission *the advancement of theological education and the work of the minister as pastor, preacher, and teacher.* Intern training is not to be viewed as a transient but a continuing undertaking; hence, only those students are to be enrolled in it for whom there is adequate seminary staff, suitable intern situations, and assurance of financial support. And because intern training is costly in man-hours and money, neither seminaries and their affiliated churches nor all the regular donors to seminary education are ever likely to be able to raise more than a part of the necessary funds. For in addition to the somewhat staggering sum required to enable interns to live, yet more money is needed to employ an additional faculty member to supervise each group of six to ten students. Even though doctoral candidates are secured and paid nominal salaries for this work, the cost will not be a trifle.

It would seem that seminaries supported by their respective denominations are in a favored position to institute pastoral intern training. Independent and university-related schools might well work through the American Association of Theological Schools to secure foundation funds and establish programs in various sections of the country, each one representing a co-operative enterprise

sponsored by neighboring schools. But it would be disad-
vantageous to seminaries and churches alike, and to the
cause of pastoral training, if money were given contingent
upon the raising of a matching sum. Already there is too
much of this sort of bargaining between educational institutions and donors, and while it may appear presumptu-
ous for a school to look the proverbial gift horse in the
mouth, if the horse is too weak to bear the burden that
necessarily only a single horse can carry, it is the better
part of wisdom politely to refuse to accept him. Indubi-
tably, the financing of educational institutions that have to
rely on volunteer gifts is an altogether different proposition from financing tax-supported institutions. State and
Federal grants to public schools, made on the basis of a
local community's agreeing to raise a stated share of the
total sum needed, have no counterpart in private and religious domains. Unfortunately foundations frequently dis-
regard this fact, and with disappointing results. Indeed,
there are independent universities that have been out of
pocket precisely *because* they received certain grants from
philanthropic foundations and business corporations. The
reason is that in securing proportionate or matching funds
from regular contributors, universities are thereby forced
to divert money from other essential needs.

It is the routine followed by foundations that works
against the recipient of their bounties. Nowadays the routine goes something like this: " We allocate money only
for new ventures, for what is old must not be very good if
you have trouble maintaining it. Yet not so much a new
venture as a study of a proposed new venture really at-
tracts us. Make us a novel proposition and if it's close to
our hearts (and clearly in the public interest), we might
be willing to give you half of what you require — not quite

half, though, because you'll have to absorb the overhead costs. And if, after scientific study, your project seems to warrant being put into operation, we would be open to another memorandum stating the cost of a pilot plan — a short-term program, you understand, at the conclusion of which you would of course be expected to find other resources for its continuation."

If this be a caricature, perhaps it correctly delineates facets of organized philanthropy's routine. Certainly it is fair to say that what is often overlooked is the fact that an educational institution may already know what needs to be done, in which case an elaborate study is both superfluous and a waste of money. And as for pilot projects, it must be observed that a pilot light on a stove is a most deceptive contrivance, unless there is also an open pipeline to a steady supply of gas. Dean Jacques Barzun, of Columbia University, has some sparkling commentaries to offer on this general subject,[33] but a university's difficulties are minor compared to those of seminaries, especially seminaries unattached either to denominations or universities.

Nor is this the whole story. Unlike universities and major colleges, schools of theology have relatively few alumni, and who among them ever reaches affluence that enables him to endow an undertaking of his school? And with few exceptions, when substantial gifts are made by business and philanthropic foundations to theological education, the strong university-related divinity schools are the beneficiaries. Thus is Scripture fulfilled: " To him who has will more be given." This is said not to complain but simply to make an observation of considerable import; for assuredly the foundations have conscientious administrators, for the most part committed to policies of disbursement based on careful study. But theirs is a power status, readily responsive to another kind of power inherent in a few schools of theology. This is to be expected and, in a measure, accepted as a legitimate bias of the executors of wealth. Yet there are those of us who would say: " Gentlemen, we beseech you by your own bowels of mercy, get yourselves a new routine! And do recall the homely truth that all that's glamorous isn't necessarily better. Consider thinking men, wherever they may be found, who with vision of excellence might just be more nearly correct about what needs to be done than a company of researchers in the behavioral sciences. Look them in the eye and if the gleam there is not too fanatical, take a risk with them; like as not you'd be tossing more money to the winds, but who knows but that these might be the winds of heaven? "

It is salutary that foundations and churches show no inclination to rely heavily on loan systems for seminarians, similar to the one for future schoolteachers set up in 1958 by the Federal Government. This national education act does less than justice to public educators, and it suggests no fitting parallel for aiding seminarians; for professionals whose income — on the average — will never permit more than frugal support of their families, ought not to be shackled to years of paying off a loan.

For every grant to phases of ministerial education all theological schools are grateful. And once the whole ministry of the church gains due recognition, more and better informed donors will ensure the training of seminary graduates as pastors, preachers, and teachers. This training is a fundamental need of theological education and a basic opportunity within Protestantism.

9

A Church Curriculum

A CURRICULUM denotes formulation of a series of courses deemed adequate to fulfill a governing purpose for teaching and learning. But the minute that formulation takes place danger arises that the curriculum will be viewed as fixed and final; fixed it may be — provisionally, but final it cannot be. For refinement, if not drastic revision, is always in order. This is true for two main reasons: first, a course of study that is vital simply has to be responsive, therefore adaptable, to the needs of persons for whom it is designed; and second, no one knows enough to say with complete confidence that this is it and this is the way it has to be. Hence, it is the better part of wisdom to be somewhat tentative with respect to any curriculum. At the same time, it becomes necessary to conceive a sequence of courses that make for coherence and unity. This is the task that constantly occupies national curriculum committees and some denominations are having good results. Careful students often find that a curriculum based on materials drawn from several sources is preferable to any one publisher's series. The reader may safely conclude, from study of this book, that who is doing the teaching is even more important than the textbooks used. To the pastor of any one of several denominations perhaps the most helpful advice I could give would be: "Take your denominational curriculum and adapt it to your teaching, not limiting yourself to it." But because other pastors desire a wider selection of texts, in this chapter I offer a curriculum outline subject to revision and amplification according to a local church's situation and the pastor-teacher's resourcefulness.

Recall once again that the purpose of church education is growth in grace and knowledge of Jesus Christ. Under this general purpose certain objectives are stated here for each age level, and under these the teacher must work out specific aims for each class session, keeping in mind the educational ideal of having still further aims pertinent for meeting the needs of each child. Reversing the order and starting with the child outward toward the overarching purpose for church-sponsored teaching and learning, it may be said that aims are immediate steps — class session after class session — toward discernible goals (objectives), which give the pupil, the teacher, and the class as a whole their bearing as they seek to realize the stated purpose of their educational enterprise. And the fruits of this experience become more or less evident to the persons involved. Furthermore, in church education, in so far as knowledge is acquired — information and facts — it can be measured just as knowledge derived from study of other subject matter can be measured. A Protestant's concern is not *whether* learning should take place in the church but *how* it is to occur, and *what* is to be learned. For even more than democracy, Protestantism requires a literate and informed constituency. By "learning" I mean "informed living"; for it profits nothing if acquirement of information about the meaning and truth of God in Christ stops short of changing a person's values and conduct. Indeed, the new person in Christ is the product of our central purpose to foster growth in grace and in knowledge. Growth in grace means growth *by* grace — the enabling power of God channeled through loving and competent teachers who enter into effective relationship with novices. This process is the *how* of church education that lies behind any organization, systematic courses of study, and methods of teaching. It is the heartbeat of nurture in Christ. But hardly less significant is the content of teaching-learning, for what we learn we become. Hence the *what* of church education has to be faced with utmost seriousness.

Now obviously what is taught must be graded to the learner's level of readiness for appropriation. Only so can it meet his intellectual, social-emotional, and spiritual needs. And because education is a growth process it should be seen whole, from beginning to end. For the very young, relations established by acceptance and love, on the teacher's part, constitute the foundation essential for growth of persons all through life. And whatever is to be said about the indispensability of guided experience for the nursery child must also be said for learners at every age. Always the curriculum is to be so fashioned that it enables the child to know, or at least to sense, that as he studies to show himself approved unto God his most basic needs are being met. In some respects, it is impossible to be entirely successful in stating objectives suitable for a given child, or even for his age level. Yet the attempt must be made. The outline in each of the several age levels is divided into headings: (1) characteristics and needs of the learner; (2) objectives; (3) theme and content; (4) evaluation.

Seen at a glance the curriculum for each of the age levels includes:

NURSERY

1st Semester: God's Big Family
2d Semester: God's Big Family

KINDERGARTEN

1st Semester: Growing in the Church
2d Semester: Growing in the Church

PRIMARY

Grade 1 1st Semester: Learning and Living in God's World
2d Semester: Learning and Living in God's World

Grade 2 1st Semester: God and Jesus
2d Semester: God and Jesus

LOWER JUNIOR

Grade 3 1st Semester: Worship at Church
2d Semester: Old Testament Stories

Grade 4 1st Semester: People God Chose
2d Semester: Heroes, Past and Present

UPPER JUNIOR

Grade 5 1st Semester: Churches in Our Town
2d Semester: The Story of The Christian Church

Grade 6 1st Semester: The Life of Christ
2d Semester: The New Testament

JUNIOR HIGH

Grade 7 1st Semester: "About Myself"
2d Semester: Christian Heritage

Grade 8 1st Semester: Church History
2d Semester: Christian Faith

Grade 9 1st Semester: Paul's Mission
2d Semester: Missions Today

SENIOR HIGH

Grade 10 1st Semester: Prophetic Religion
2d Semester: Comparative Religion
Grade 11 1st Semester: Religion in Art and Music
2d Semester: Social Ethics
Grade 12 1st Semester: Introduction to Theology
2d Semester: Christian Ethics

JUNIOR COLLEGE

1st Year 1st Semester: The Meaning of Life
2d Semester: Biblical Faith
2d Year 1st Semester: Philosophy of Religion
2d Semester: Christian Marriage

ADULTS
Elective Courses and Informal Study Groups

It is to be understood that the outline may be followed in the church that either adopts the pastor-teacher idea *in toto* or continues with the Sunday school and lay teaching up through the fourth grade. And it should be stated that although every book here listed is not necessary for good teaching, each one should be examined if not purchased.

NURSERY
Three-year-olds
Theme: GOD'S BIG FAMILY

1. *Characteristics and Needs*
    The child is ready to venture outside the home. He wants to be with children his age. Play is his natural

mode of expression and means of learning. He needs mothering but also opportunity to experiment with his developing powers in novel and social situations. An imitator, he relies on the human environment to guide him and is responsive to limitations set by the teacher, to attitude, to tone of voice, and to the total physical setting. Necessarily egocentric, he can be directed and is in the early stages of developing a conscience. Guidance rather than direct instruction is the clue to helping him learn. His basic need is for healthy emotional development, the necessary foundation for spiritual growth.

2. *Objectives*

(*a*) To enable the child to experience acceptance and love in relationship with the teacher, hence to learn respect for the self; (*b*) to enjoy a permissive situation and therefore freedom to play creatively; (*c*) to enter into co-operative social experiences, finding therein some realization of what it means to belong in the church, the family of God; (*d*) to feel confident and to sense that God is loving and his world is good.

3. *Theme and Content*

Some awareness that God is love is gained through constructive nursery experiences. The content for the year is precisely a sense of unity with the people of God's church, unity derived through relationship with a loving teacher, and with peers who — like the individual child — are learning to share, take turns, hold the self in check for the sake of another. Simple stories and songs, good phonograph music,[34] experimentation with paints and clay, use of toys, and care of plants and pets, rest, short prayers and grace said over milk and cookies, and occasional visits to the sanctuary, all these constitute the substance of what is being experienced, consequently learned.

BOOKS FOR THE TEACHER

When They Are Three, by Sara G. Klein and Elizabeth C. Gardner. The Westminster Press, 1956.

Religious Living with Nursery Children in Home and Church, by Phoebe M. Anderson. The Pilgrim Press, 1956.

Consider the Children How They Grow (revised edition), by E. M. Manwell and S. L. Fahs. The Beacon Press, Inc., 1951.

BOOKS TO USE WITH THE CHILDREN

Martin and Judy, Vol. I (revised edition), by Verna Hills Bayley. The Beacon Press, Inc., 1959.

Martin and Judy Songs, edited by Edith Lovell Thomas. The Beacon Press, Inc., 1948.

Prayers for Little Children, by Mary Alice Jones. Rand McNally & Company, 1937.

A Little Book of Singing Graces, by Jeanette Perkins Brown. Abingdon Press, 1946.

Curriculum reading books published by The Westminster Press.

4. *Evaluation*

Although a formal report on the child's progress may not be desired, close observation enables the teacher to determine whether or not the child is achieving the stated objectives. An anecdotal record (see Chapter Four in *Religious Living with Nursery Children in Home and Church*) is an effective means of appraising the child's experiences. The gist of the record may be transmitted informally to parents.

KINDERGARTEN
Four- and Five-year-olds
Theme: GROWING IN THE CHURCH

1. *Characteristics and Needs*

Dr. Arnold Gesell and his associates have reported at length [35] on the characteristics of young children. Unfortunately their findings are popularly interpreted as norms for a given age level. Thus many speak of the " out of bounds " four-year-old and the " conforming " five-year-old. As covering phrases go, these serve fairly well with respect to some children. Developmentally there is a wide range of behavior and capacity to learn between the child just turned four and the child nearing his sixth birthday, and many churches divide the two ages for classes. The fours may differ little in ability from a good many three-year-olds and the fives may already be interested in learning to read, therefore bored with the " baby stuff " of nursery school. Even allowing for less divergence between the fours and fives, it is noted that the younger are primarily questioners (just to keep the talk going) and experimenters with language — silly talk, nonsense words, including the unprintable (generally nothing to them but sounds) — while the older ask questions in order to gain information and are generally more sedate. The two groups differ in physical development as well as social poise, the more mature fives responding to brief instruction and conversation that answer their questions and stimulate wondering about the world around them. But the kindergarten child still needs freedom like that enjoyed in the nursery class. And because his range of interest has expanded and his imagination increased he probably has more fears than earlier. This is the case whether or not he voices them.

2. *Objectives*

The same as for the nursery; plus (a) pupil and teacher sharing in the wonder of nature and in the child's fears so that God may be thought of as Creator and as a refuge in time of trouble; (b) learning to pray and sing; (c) participating in seasonal observances and in the celebration of Christmas and Easter; (d) experiencing worship in occasional family services in the sanctuary.

3. *Theme and Content*

" Growing in the Church " starts with the world the child experiences and imagines. He confuses God with magic and is dependent upon adults for religious ideas; hence, it is important that good ingredients be brought into his experiences: practice in being a helper; expressing thanks to the God of love who, though somewhat like loving parents and friends, is understood by the child to be even more powerful; learning to tend plants and animals, part of God's creation; looking at good pictures; listening to poems, stories, and tone poems in great music; participating in family worship in the sanctuary.

BOOKS FOR THE TEACHER

Teaching the Youngest, by Mabel Louise Culkin. The Macmillan Company, 1949.

Father to the Child, by Everett S. Ostrovsky. G. P. Putnam's Sons, 1959.

Religion in the Kindergarten, by Rosemary K. Roorbach. Harper & Brothers, 1949.

Christmas and Its Customs, By Christina Hole. M. Barrows & Company, Inc., 1958.

BOOKS TO USE WITH THE CHILDREN

Martin and Judy, Vols. II and III (revised editions), by Verna Hills Bayley. The Beacon Press, Inc., 1959.

Holiday Storybook. Child Study Association of America. The Thomas Y. Crowell Co., 1952.

Told Under the Blue Umbrella. Association for Childhood Education. The Macmillan Company, 1933.

For a Child: Great Poems Old and New, collected by Wilma McFarland and illustrated by Ninon. The Westminster Press, 1947.

Tell Me About Prayer, by Mary Alice Jones. Rand McNally & Company, 1948.

In the Morning: Twenty Bible Verses, pictured by Louise Drew. Abingdon Press, 1947.

When the Little Child Wants to Sing. The Westminster Press, 1935.

Martin and Judy Songs, edited by Edith Lovell Thomas. The Beacon Press, Inc., 1948.

4. *Evaluation*

The same as with nursery children. In addition it is desirable to recognize the child's progress by written commentaries sent to parents. This is the custom of good private and public kindergartens that report on group relations, handwork, special interests, language usage, and more. For the church kindergarten there should be an item dealing with religious interests and any possible fears needing parents' attention. For a report form, see below under Grade 1.

PRIMARY
Grade 1
Theme: LEARNING AND LIVING IN GOD'S WORLD

1. *Characteristics and Needs*

In *The Child from Five to Ten,* Gesell and Ilg draw much the same contrast between the six- and seven-year-olds, on the one hand, and the four- and five-year-olds, on the other. But whereas the kindergarteners fare better in a relatively unstructured class experience, the sixes and sevens need detailed work. They are school people and their main business is reading and writing, and learning to figure — in the case of the church class, learning not arithmetic but to figure the difference between the real and the imagined in the religious realm. Literalist that he is, the school beginner is getting down to particulars: differentiating objects, finding out who will take care of him if his mother dies, distinguishing between God and the devil, speculating about where God and heaven are, specifying for what he is thankful down to the last carrot and cherished toy, and expecting God to grant specific prayer requests. The child is at once trustful and a bit skeptical, religious and almost wholly self-centered. But this is a transitional stage and he is beginning to grow out of immediate concerns, abide by rules, and assume a more responsible place in society. He wants to live up to the rules and " be good," but if too rigidly controlled, he resorts to deception and theft, partly to escape punishment, partly because his emotional needs may drive him to deviation, and partly because he has not yet completed learning the difference between fantasy and fact. He is a thinker and wants to know about himself and his growth in relation to other growing things. Although he is not yet ready to study people and events in distant time and place, he can profit by brief introduction to them.

2. *Objectives*

(*a*) In group conversation to wonder about God and his creation; (*b*) to observe animal babies and the care of human infants, and picture them in drawing, conversation, and play acting; (*c*) to know in some detail the story of Jesus' birth and construct a manger scene at Christmas time; (*d*) to learn to pray the Lord's Prayer from memory; (*e*) to enjoy books on the browsing table (see below) and to memorize Bible verses in *Small Rain;* (*f*) to memorize the Ten Commandments and study the Golden Rule (in relation to rules the class draws up for guiding their conduct at church, home, and school); (*g*) to compose prayer poems and look ahead toward memorization of Bible poems (see second and third grade memory work).

3. *Theme and Content*

Two themes run through the first grade: the wonder of growing things and learning right living. The content emerges from the children's experience, their thinking and imagining, and from portions of the Bible. Two quite opposed theological positions — that of Seabury and that of Beacon materials — are represented in the recommended books. Some teachers will prefer to use the publications of only one of these positions. Others will find help in both and keep them in fruitful tension. Actually children at all ages learn " naturally," *and* by indoctrination; the one procedure without the other is misguiding. But it must be recognized that harmonizing the two requires high achievement by the teacher.

BOOKS FOR THE TEACHER

Wonder and Faith in the First Grade. A manual. The Seabury Press, Inc., 1958.

Exploring Nature and Life with Five- and Six-year-olds, by Edith F. Hunter. The Beacon Press, Inc., 1951.

The Holy Bible, Revised Standard Version. Thomas Nelson & Sons, 1952.

Exploring the Child's World, by Helen Parkhurst. Appleton-Century-Crofts, Inc., 1951.

Let's Play a Story, by Elizabeth Allstrom. Friendship Press, 1957.

Activities in Child Education, by Elizabeth M. Lobingier. The Pilgrim Press, 1950.

The Storyteller in Religious Education, by Jeanette Perkins Brown. The Pilgrim Press, 1951.

Hymns for Primary Worship. The Westminster Press, 1946.

BOOKS TO USE WITH THE CHILDREN

The Family Finds Out, by Edith F. Hunter. The Beacon Press, Inc., 1951.

Animal Babies, by Alice Day Pratt. The Beacon Press, Inc., 1959.

A Brand New Baby, by Margaret A. Stanger. The Beacon Press, Inc., 1955.

Small Rain, by Jessie Orton Jones. The Viking Press, 1943.

My Own Book of Prayers, by Mary Alice Jones. Rand McNally & Company, 1938.

4. *Evaluation*

Paralleling the frequency with which public schools

send reports home (three or four times during the year), the church teacher should make a written evaluation of pupils. An example of a suitable form follows.

PUPIL'S CHURCH CLASS REPORT

For period ending _____

Name _____ Grade ____

Course of Study _____

Times absent ____   Times tardy ____

1. *Participation in group activities*
   a. Conversation and planning:

   b. Stories, singing, and worship:

   c. Class or group projects:

   d. Other items:

2. *Individual Accomplishment*
   a. Special interests:

b. Goals reached:

(Here the teacher's record book makes possible accurate appraisal of the child according to the stated objectives for the year's work. Also, mimeographed goal sheets can be shared with parents in private conferences, but not until the child is in the fourth or fifth grade is it wise to provide him with the sheet, and then the teacher must recognize individual differences and allow for varying rates of learning.)

c. Area for further work:

(Some deficiencies are better mentioned orally, but comments like this may be written: " Jack needs help in distinguishing between his and others' property." Or, " Sue should work for neatness in writing and drawing.")

3. *Awareness of class purposes and response to them:*

4. *Pupil's expressed desires or needs:*

5. *Research, reports, essays (for sixth grade and older students):*

6. *Summary rating (for third-graders and up):*

EXCELLENT _____; GOOD _____; SATISFACTORY _____;
UNSATISFACTORY _____

_____, Teacher

(Signed)

Grade 2
Theme: GOD AND JESUS

1. *Characteristics and Needs*

While recognizing that first- and second-grade children live primarily in the "here and now," account must also be taken of their growing outreach in space and time. (One seven-year-old often prayed " And thank you, God, for space too.") Their preoccupation with people and life around them allows for a glimmer of the long ago, though the ancient is confused with the contemporary. And because they feel the recurrent birth and death of Jesus, especially at Christmas and Easter, they need to be introduced directly and factually to these and other Gospel events, without sentimentalizing or dramatics on the part of the teacher.

Characteristically, the second-grader enjoys doing his work, carrying out learning tasks. He seems to grasp rather fully how essential it is that he master the printed page; and actually both his future success as a student and citizen and his emotional development hinge upon reading ability. Around the age of seven, wonder and insightful thinking assume a scope surprising to most adults, for the child usually opens himself but briefly to adults. Needing to share his big thoughts, he may not do so because thoughtless grownups laugh at him. Wanting help in getting things straight about God and all mystery, the child welcomes sensitive understanding by a teacher and likely falls in love with such a one for life. Well-conceived routine suits the seven-year-old. He likes rhythm and is capable of memory work and elementary performance in a verse-speaking choir. Perhaps he responds better and benefits more

from formal worship than has been realized in the recent past.

2. *Objectives*

(*a*) To develop some understanding that God is Love
and Spirit and that his Son Jesus came to show people
the right way to live; (*b*) to become familiar with certain New Testament events: Jesus at twelve in the
Temple; Jesus teaching by telling stories; the envy
shown Jesus by religious leaders; Jesus' betrayal, death,
and resurrection; the disciples' recovery and the beginning of the church; (*c*) to dramatize such stories as the
good Samaritan and the lost coin; (*d*) to learn worship
through use of hymns, prayers, stories, and memorization of Ps. 1; 24; 90; 100; 121.

3. *Theme and Content*

Interwoven with the Biblical content is the theme of
learning to grow, as Jesus did, in favor with God. Instruction inheres in engaging in interesting and varied
activities. For instance, in planning a worship service,
the class may compose a prayer poem, memorize a
psalm and use it in a verse-speaking choir; or, by way
of participating in a missionary or social service project
of the church, the class can make up picture books
that tell the story of their understanding of God and
Jesus.

Memory work should come through enjoyment of
rhythm and group repetition, with little drill or demand
by teacher or parents. In churches that separate classes
into groups according to fast and slow learners, it is
easier to fit memory and other learning tasks to the
child's level of readiness.

Miss Parkhurst's *Exploring the Child's World,* recommended for the first-grade teacher, should also be used by teachers of the second grade and others, for it demonstrates the importance of knowing the *extent* and the *what* of the school age child's ability to think. The Seabury manual, *My Place in God's World*, suggests methods of working with young learners. Sections of this book are worth considerable study by the teacher.

It is regrettable that church publishers have not kept pace with educational and commercial presses in providing suitable readers for children of early school age. However, some second-graders can read at least parts of the church books published for use with them.

BOOKS FOR THE TEACHER

My Place in God's World. A manual. The Seabury Press, Inc., 1958.

The Story of Jesus for Young People, by Walter Russell Bowie. Charles Scribner's Sons, 1937.

Creative Dramatics in Home, School, and Community, by R. G. Lease and G. B. Siks. Harper & Brothers, 1952.

BOOKS TO USE WITH THE CHILDREN

Jesus, Stories for Children, by James D. Smart. The Westminster Press, 1948.

Good News to Tell, by Florence M. Taylor. The Westminster Press, 1949.

The Wondrous Works of God, illustrated by Symeon Shimin. The Seabury Press, Inc., 1958.

Always Growing, by Elizabeth M. Manwell. The Beacon Press, Inc., 1957.

4. *Evaluation*

Use the Pupil's Church Class Report.

LOWER JUNIOR
Grade 3
First Semester: WORSHIP AT CHURCH
Second Semester: OLD TESTAMENT STORIES

1. *Characteristics and Needs*

About the age of eight or nine a child's conscience normally is rather well developed. He is no longer the center of the universe, for he has the capacity to be concerned with others. This is the beginning of altruism. His understanding of God reaches a new dimension, and he is capable of a more formal kind of instruction in worship, including the principles of stewardship and Christian giving. Interest in primitive people induces re-enactment of folkways. In public school, units of study may reconstruct American Indian life or colonial America and the children dwell for a time in tents, huts, or splendid houses. Thus in the church class tent dwelling can take the Israelite form of the nomadic period in Bible history. Being able now to distinguish between mere story and history, between what writers thought and what was more probably true, the third-grader is ready for an introduction to selected Old Testament stories. Despite a decidedly improved time concept (partly denoted by his learning to tell clock time) the eight-year-old yet conceives of a thousand years as but a day. There is advantage in this, for he can enjoy Biblical figures as his contemporaries while yet speaking of them as at least as old as Granddad.

Money now takes on fresh significance for the child, hence his need to gain elementary conception of Christian stewardship. But the use to which his contribution to the church is put must be made very concrete to him.

He wants to know more than he is generally told about "the poor people" to whom charity is directed.

2. *Objectives*

First semester: (*a*) To gain elementary understanding of forms of worship used in the local church and — as an act of worship — to learn to give a part of one's allowance to the church; (*b*) to learn church hymns and stories about the writers; (*c*) to read great prayers and compose original ones. Second semester: (*a*) To memorize Ps. 8; 23; 46; 67; 84; 130; 150; (*b*) to become familiar with stories of Creation; Abraham's call; events in the lives of Jacob and Joseph; Moses and the deliverance from Egypt; the founding and fall of the kingdom, exile, and return; (*c*) to participate in class projects, music, and dramatics.

3. *Theme and Content*

Divided into semesters, work for the fall deals with congregational worship and for the spring with Old Testament stories and events. This year of study might prove too taxing to the child unless he has abundant expressional activity. The teacher is advised to keep in touch with the kind of project work done in a good modern public or private school, for thereby it becomes apparent that mastery of content is facilitated by class planning and activity guided by the teacher. Less memory work is to be expected of pupils who are poor readers; for superior minds added work is desirable.

BOOKS FOR THE FIRST SEMESTER

FOR THE TEACHER

The Gospel in Hymns, by Albert E. Bailey. Charles Scribner's Sons, 1950.

The Psalms and Their Meaning for Today, by Samuel Terrien. The Bobbs-Merrill Company, Inc., 1952.

The Psalms as Christian Praise, by R. B. Y. Scott. World Christian Books. Association Press, 1958.

As Children Worship, by Jeanette E. Perkins. The Pilgrim Press, 1936.

Here's How and When, by Armilda Keiser. Friendship Press, 1952.

Hymns for Primary Worship. The Westminster Press, 1946, and the local church's hymnal.

FOR THE PUPIL

Our Prayers and Praise. The Seabury Press, Inc., 1957. (For adaptation to various denominations' use and a guide to the pupil as he develops his own book of prayers.)

BOOKS FOR THE SECOND SEMESTER

FOR THE TEACHER

Understanding the Old Testament, by Bernhard W. Anderson. Prentice-Hall, Inc., 1957.

The Interpreter's Bible, Vols. 1–3. Abingdon Press, 1952–1954.

The Bible Story for Boys and Girls, by Walter Russell Bowie. Abingdon Press, 1952.

Creative Dramatics in Home, School, and Community, by R. G. Lease and G. B. Siks. Harper & Brothers, 1952.

FOR THE PUPIL

Picture Dictionary of the Bible, by Ruth Tubby. Abingdon Press, 1949.

People of the Promise, by Elizabeth Honness. The Westminster Press, 1949.

And So the Wall Was Built, by Imogene M. McPherson.

The Westminster Press, 1949.

Thine Is the Glory, by Florence M. Taylor. The Westminster Press, 1948.

4. *Evaluation*

Use the Pupil's Church Class Report, including item 6.

Grade 4
First Semester: PEOPLE GOD CHOSE
Second Semester: HEROES, PAST AND PRESENT

1. *Characteristics and Needs*

Quoting Jean Piaget, the Swiss psychologist, on the moral judgment of children, Blair and Burton[36] point out that around the age of nine or ten the child begins to appraise motives or circumstances that give rise to behavior, not judging it as he did earlier in terms of black or white, wrong or right. His marked concern with justice and fair play now allows for flexibility in determining what these virtues are in a given situation. Thus the fourth-grader is advancing beyond sole reliance on adult rules and conformity to a point at which he must establish a more personal and peer-group code of conduct. Indeed, for him his peers challenge parent- and teacher-authority, and what formerly drew the child as an individual may now have to appeal to him as a member of the gang. Very likely he is captivated by major figures, the more heroic the better, whether in contemporary life or in past history. As boys gravitate toward other boys, and girls toward other girls, each group needs actual and vicarious experiences with significant persons of its own sex. Not that males always require males and females need females, as teachers and subjects of study, but some provision along these lines is desirable — particularly for boys who in our society are often thrown too much with women.

Although the fourth-grade pupil yet lacks a well-defined sense of time, he is interested in introduction to history. This fact has relevance for study of portions of the Old Testament. The pupil is ready to connect the few stories he has had in the third grade with a historic pattern broadly conceived. Traditionally, churches have given Bibles to children at the end of the third grade; to a limited extent, in the fourth grade they can use them.

2. *Objectives*

First semester: (*a*) To know the beginnings of the people chosen by God to carry his message to the world; (*b*) to gain a realistic conception of the good and bad in leaders used by God to advance his cause in history; (*c*) to review psalms previously learned and memorize Isa. 40:1-11; 52:7-10; ch. 53; 61:1-3. Second semester: (*a*) To become acquainted with heroes such as Francis of Assisi, Martin Luther, John Wesley, Gandhi, Florence Nightingale, and Albert Schweitzer; (*b*) to read biographies and discuss in class the attributes of greatness; (*c*) to dramatize episodes in the lives of heroes.

3. *Theme and Content*

The theme for the entire year is greatness in people chosen by God. It is to be recognized that because the time concept is not well developed in children until they are close to the age of puberty, chronology and subdivisions of history mean little to them. Therefore, the emphasis in the fourth grade is on the Old Testament story in broad outline, and on personalities. Care is to be exercised lest too much be expected of the pupils, or too little. The resourceful teacher will recognize that nine-year-olds should be consulted in planning units of study. They can use reference books and begin reading assigned Bible passages. During the second semester at least one new book every three or four weeks is needed for pupils' reading of biography. Choice of persons to study should be made by the teacher and class together.

BOOKS FOR THE FIRST SEMESTER

FOR THE TEACHER

Personalities of the Old Testament, by Fleming James. Charles Scribner's Sons, 1938.

The Story of the Bible (revised edition), by Walter Russell Bowie. Abingdon Press, 1954.

FOR THE PUPIL

The Holy Bible, Revised Standard Version. Thomas Nelson & Sons, 1952.

Lands of the Bible, by Samuel Terrien. A Golden Historical Atlas. Simon and Schuster, Inc., 1957.

A Promise to Keep, by James D. Smart. The Westminster Press, 1949.

BOOKS FOR THE SECOND SEMESTER

FOR THE TEACHER

(Biographies more complete than the ones listed for pupils may be consulted by the teacher.)

Let's Play a Story, by Elizabeth Allstrom. Friendship Press, 1957.

Creative Dramatics in Home, School, and Community,

by R. G. Lease and G. B. Siks. Harper & Brothers, 1952.

FOR THE PUPIL

God's Troubador: The Story of Saint Francis of Assisi, by Sophie Jewett. The Thomas Y. Crowell Co., 1957.

Martin Luther, by M. Y. McNeer and L. K. Ward. Abingdon Press, 1953.

Landing of the Pilgrims, by James Daugherty. Landmark Book. Random House, Inc., 1950.

John Wesley, by M. Y. McNeer and L. K. Ward. Abingdon Press, 1958.

Armed with Courage, by M. Y. McNeer and L. K. Ward. Abingdon Press, 1957.

The Story of Louis Pasteur, by Alida Sims Malkus. Grosset & Dunlap, Inc., 1952.

There Go the Conquerors, by Basil Mathews. Round Table Press, 1943.

The Story of Albert Schweitzer, by Anita Daniel. World Landmark Book. Random House, Inc., 1957.

Theirs Is the Kingdom, by Jack M. MacLeod. The Westminster Press, 1959.

4. *Evaluation*

Use the Pupil's Church Class Report and confer with the child and his parents.

UPPER JUNIOR
Grade 5
First Semester: CHURCHES IN OUR TOWN
Second Semester: THE STORY OF THE CHRISTIAN CHURCH

1. *Characteristics and Needs*

Interested in accumulating facts and finding acceptance with a few mates of the same sex and age, the fifth-grade pupil usually responds better to a church class if the teacher is something of a club leader, willing to consult with the pupils and able to channel their ideas as the group as a whole stipulates its aims. (The ten-year-old is generally willing to formulate aims within the stated objectives of the course of study.) With all his need for increased self-reliance and his right to be consulted, the child yet wants directing. And though not until he is about eleven can he see historic connections and grasp the causal factors in society, modern or ancient, observable human customs earlier attract his attention and serve to launch him on a course of inquiry. And if the physical universe means more to the preadolescent child than a spiritual interpretation of it, humans and their social, institutional, and religious customs do mean something to him. The fifth-grader can contrast the present with the past. Furthermore, Blair and Burton state that " the average eleven-year-old child has the reading skill equal to that of the average adult." [37] When we keep in mind that a good proportion of fifth-grade pupils pass their eleventh birthday during this year, and that reading for enjoyment is a skill that the normally developed child of this age has possessed for a year or two, then we can realize how little church teachers in the past have expected of him. Certainly the fifth-grader needs to have his intellectual and potential spiritual capacities challenged by the church class. He has reached a critical period when he demands more than the trivial.

2. *Objectives*

First semester: (*a*) To find out about "the church across the street," both for the sake of satisfying curiosity and understanding better one's own church; (*b*) to begin a study of comparative religion by becoming familiar with the different ways neighbors worship. Second semester: (*a*) To make a first sustained study of church history; (*b*) to know particularly the Protestant Reformation.

3. *Theme and Content*

In the first semester " Churches in Our Town " are investigated and effort is made to understand varieties of worship. This should motivate pupils to study " The Story of the Christian Church." Handicraft is especially useful in the first semester.

BOOKS FOR THE FIRST SEMESTER

FOR THE TEACHER
> *The Great Tradition of the American Churches,* by Winthrop S. Hudson. Harper & Brothers, 1953.
> *The Story of Religion in America* (revised edition), by William W. Sweet. Harper & Brothers, 1950.

FOR THE PUPIL
> *The Church Across the Street,* by Sophia Lyon Fahs and Reginald D. Manwell. The Beacon Press, Inc., 1947.
> *One God: The Ways We Worship Him,* by Florence Mary Fitch. Lothrop, Lee & Shepard Co., Inc., 1944.
> *Make It Yourself! Handicraft for Boys and Girls,* by Bernice Wells Carlson. Abingdon Press, 1950.

BOOKS FOR THE SECOND SEMESTER

FOR THE TEACHER
> *The Goodly Company.* A manual. The Seabury Press, Inc., 1958.

A History of Christianity, by Kenneth Scott Latourette. Harper & Brothers, 1953.

Here I Stand: A Life of Martin Luther, by Roland Bainton. A Mentor Book, 1950.

FOR THE PUPIL

Fire Upon the Earth: The Story of the Christian Church, by Norman F. Langford. The Westminster Press, 1950.

Traveling the Way, by McGowen and Sydnor. The Seabury Press, Inc., 1958.

4. *Evaluation*

In addition to the usual report to parents, from this age up through junior high, the teacher should provide each child with a goal sheet on which he makes a record of his work. Under the stated objectives for the year, specific aims are listed and checked off as accomplished by the pupil, for example: visit a Quaker meeting house for worship____; make a Menorah____; write a brief story on "My Favorite Protestant Reformer"____.

Grade 6
First Semester: THE LIFE OF CHRIST
Second Semester: THE NEW TESTAMENT

1. *Characteristics and Needs*

A wise schoolmaster has said that sixth-graders should be treated in a somewhat offhand manner. For many, this age is characterized by the ambivalence of wanting to grow up and become one's self, and wanting to hold on to familiar relationships of childhood, when parents were king and queen and all that was necessary for the loyal subject was to comply with established codes. Yet for some time the perceptive child has had indubitable evidence that parents and other adults are not without flaws. Thus loyalty and honest appraisal may vie within the child and cause him considerable turbulence, which sometimes erupts in nightmares or overt rebellion against adults. No longer is the child simply a child and he may insist on being referred to as a " subteen." Moreover, in our society, pubescence seems to be occurring somewhat earlier on the average; and social development is speeded up by dancing classes, coeducational schools, and incessant exposure of the child—by television and the press —to the ways of teen-agers and adults. Hardly is there time any more for a child to be a child and he, like older people, is aware that traditional moorings have slipped. Yet he both needs and seeks moral and religious anchorage. In churches practicing believers' baptism he is likely to have a conversion experience and join the church; or he may join in order to find social and personal satisfactions, for he is a practitioner of joining things: teams, clubs, gangs. Actually he needs to be close to his church and to identify himself with the followers of Christ.

There is considerable evidence that the preadolescent can generalize about as well as the young adolescent. Usually a reader, in varied and wide fields, the sixth-grader is capable of consulting encyclopedias and carrying on research in an area of his interest. Although intelligence is not yet fully developed in the eleven-year-old, the maturation process has advanced his powers of conceptualization and his ability to feel larger loyalties than hitherto. If a study of Swiss children, made by Piaget and Weil,[38] may be taken as reliable for American children, our sixth-graders can include at least the nation in their in-group or circle of attachment. This is in sharp contrast to the capacity of children only a year or two younger, who cannot embrace one loyalty within another. The sixth-grader is glad to have quiet acknowledgment of whatever skills he possesses and to respond to a detached but friendly teacher alert to guide his growth. Not only boys but also girls need a good male teacher.

2. *Objectives*

First semester: (*a*) To read and understand the earliest Gospel, the book of Mark; (*b*) to "ventilate" perplexities, doubts, and rebellious feelings of whatever cause. Second semester: (*a*) To study other great passages from the New Testament, notably Matt., chs. 5; 6; 7; Acts, chs. 22; 26:2-23; Rom., ch. 12; I Cor., ch. 13; Heb., ch. 11; I John, chs. 1; 2; 3:1-3; and learn the historic conditions out of which they came; (*b*) to find in these passages, and the class experience as a whole, realistic guidance in problems of living and in giving loyalty to Christ and universal man above all else; (*c*) to know the order and circumstances in which the New Testament books were written.

3. *Theme and Content*

Mark's Gospel and the individual's response to the Person of Christ constitute the content of the first semester. In the second, examination is made of the way in which the New Testament spoke to the problems of the early Christians, and today speaks to persons' needs. Commenting on the Piaget and Weil study, Allport observes that "most children never enlarge their sense of belonging beyond the ties of family, city, nation. The reason seems to be that those with whom the child lives, and whose judgment he mirrors, do not do so." [39] Allport concludes that loyalty to a circle larger than the nation can be learned. From the sixth grade on, at many points in this curriculum, opportunity is given the church teacher to help his students form attachment to the universal above the national, to the Christ of the Gospels rather than to the Christ of a sect.

BOOKS FOR THE FIRST SEMESTER

FOR THE TEACHER

Deciding for Myself. A manual. The Seabury Press, Inc., 1958.

The Interpreter's Bible, Vol. 7. Abingdon Press, 1951.

The Earliest Gospel, by Frederick C. Grant. Abingdon Press, 1943.

FOR THE PUPIL

The Son of God: Readings from the Gospel According to St. Mark, with background and information, by E. A. Weld and W. Sydnor. The Seabury Press, Inc., 1958.

A Life of Jesus, by Edgar J. Goodspeed. Harper & Brothers, 1950.

The Gospels Translated into Modern English, by J. B. Phillips. The Macmillan Company, 1953.

BOOKS FOR THE SECOND SEMESTER

FOR THE TEACHER

Understanding the New Testament, by H. C. Kee and F. W. Young. Prentice-Hall, Inc., 1957.

The Story of the Bible, by Edgar J. Goodspeed. University of Chicago Press, 1936.

FOR THE PUPIL

The Bible Story for Boys and Girls: New Testament, by Walter Russell Bowie. Abingdon Press, 1952.

Lands of the Bible, by Samuel Terrien. A Golden Historical Atlas. Simon and Schuster, Inc., 1957.

The Graphic Bible, by Lewis Browne. The Macmillan Company, 1951.

4. *Evaluation*

With this age level the teacher fills out item 5 on the Pupil's Church Class Report, "Research, reports, essays," for work along these lines is appropriate for the sixth-grader as well as for older students.

JUNIOR HIGH
Grade 7
First Semester: "ABOUT MYSELF"
Second Semester: CHRISTIAN HERITAGE

1. *Characteristics and Needs*

The school system of many American communities requires a decided shift from the sixth grade to the first year of junior high. The child goes to another building where he is responsible to several teachers instead of one. In various classrooms he pursues a curriculum within the general curriculum, one specifically graded to his ability. Some students are mature enough to study science as an adult might; they may already know where they are going academically and occupationally. Others are less mature, perhaps careless or indifferent, or clearly inferior learners. The tendency now is for all to be much concerned with the peer group and social relations, and with their bodies. The physically less well developed child is likely to be unhappy and the most advanced adolescent to be unfamiliar with his newly acquired physique. Whether overtly placid or erratic the seventh-grader needs to come to terms with authority. Understanding himself is a task that has to be learned in a social setting, and this he is disposed to do. Hence he perceives the importance of education for school and community citizenship, with its attendant experiences of clubs, school councils, and academic interest groups. Similarly, he is more or less aware that understanding the moral and religious self needs to be learned in the religious community, the church. And while junior high persons commonly flock to church youth groups, there is generally less inclination to take seriously formal instruction at the church. Granted that the church class may not be as worthless as the young person thinks, it is still resisted — often because the youth feels a need to resist authority in some area.

Seventh-graders do not want to be accorded full adult rights, but neither will they tolerate being patronized or treated as children. What they do want, and need, is a combination of matter-of-fact and friendly treatment by adults in authority over them. Quite simply, they desire to be respected as persons. Moreover, their maturing sense of heritage, and their place in it, causes them to be interested in varieties of religious views and how these came into being.

2. *Objectives*

First semester: (*a*) To understand physiological growth and its bearing on social and religious development; (b) to explore latent and overt resentment toward authority — in home, school, community, and church — and find a sound basis for becoming morally and spiritually responsible persons. Second semester: (a) To study historic and social differences among the major denominations; (b) to learn the distinctive beliefs and polity of the local church.

3. *Theme and Content*

First semester study, "About Myself," goes farther than dealing with psychological and religious aspects of spiritual growth; it integrates these with knowledge about the biological and physiological. And for several reasons: the Bible never denies the body, youth today are maturing and marrying earlier, and it is the business of the Christian church to encompass that much abused phrase "the whole person." Furthermore, a weekday church class is a fitting occasion to teach the facts of life and love; seemingly more fitting than the Sunday hour in class or youth group, or the public-school class.

The second semester deals with the Christian heritage, viewed interdenominationally, and within it the distinctive structure of the local church denomination. Among primitive peoples the boy of twelve quite commonly was accorded full rights of the adult. In Western culture this is not done, but the boy and girl should at least have preparation for mature entrance into Christian community. Beyond the academic approach to this preparation the church class ought to adopt something of the mood and freedom of a responsible youth group. If possible, either an hour-and-a-half session or two one-hour sessions should be set aside each week for each class, with a part of the time reserved for business, social, and service activities under the direction of elected officers. Such a plan eliminates need for the Sunday evening youth meeting. However, in some situations the young people and the teacher may decide to keep the weekday class and youth group separate. Whatever the decision, the programs of the two ought to be unified; not only so, the group needs to be integrated in the life of the church. The seventh grade is to be looked upon as a year of preparation for personal commitment to Christ. Ordinarily in the eighth grade, full membership in his church will follow.

BOOKS FOR THE FIRST SEMESTER

FOR THE TEACHER

Why Should I? A manual. The Seabury Press, Inc., 1958.

The Adolescent Views Himself, by Ruth Strang. McGraw-Hill Book Co., Inc., 1957.

FOR THE STUDENT

About Myself, by Nevin C. Harner. Christian Education Press, 1950.

Facts of Life and Love for Teen-agers (revised edition), by Evelyn Millis Duvall. Association Press or Popular Library, 1956.

BOOKS FOR THE SECOND SEMESTER

FOR THE TEACHER

Why Should I? A manual. The Seabury Press, Inc., 1958.

The Social Sources of Denominationalism, by H. Richard Niebuhr. Meridian Books, Inc., 1954.

FOR THE STUDENT

More than Words. The Seabury Press, Inc., 1958.

How We Got Our Denominations, by Stanley I. Stuber. Association Press, 1959.

The constitution and bylaws of the local church.

4. *Evaluation*

In step with public-school practice, the church teacher will use suitable group and individual projects, together with short essays and quizzes to help the student master the courses of study. An evaluative conference should be held each semester with each student and due care given to filling out the Church Class Report.

Grade 8
First Semester: CHURCH HISTORY
Second Semester: CHRISTIAN FAITH

1. *Characteristics and Needs*

Adults often think junior high people are irresponsible and difficult to work with. When it is recalled that adolescents are deeply involved in growth changes — physical, social, emotional, and ethical — in addition to increasingly difficult curricular and extracurricular demands, it is easy to understand why they may behave erratically. Each individual's pattern of development is uniquely his, but in general it may be said that eighth-graders are concerned with heterosexual adjustment, gaining social status among their peers while enjoying progressively more freedom from parental control, and with orienting themselves to their expanding intellectual horizon. Swift alternation is likely to occur from adultlike behavior to childishness, and the youth is torn between the need to perceive what kind of person he is and his desire to embrace larger concerns. Indeed, he is beginning to look for a cause to serve, not merely unifying his resources but discovering a master sentiment and a purpose for his life.[40] Normally he is capable of seeing connections between ideas and situations and, though he is primarily an activist rather than a reflective thinker, he can and does think. Both current and historic affairs interest him and he finds the world of books important. Blair and Burton quote one study showing that " the peak in variety and amount of reading done by typical boys and girls is at twelve or thirteen years" and another that found that " the height in reading interest is at age thirteen for the child of average intelligence." [41] The reference is to free reading, when the choice is the reader's rather than the teacher's. Is the youth looking for something relevant to his need, perhaps for clues about the meaning of life?

In the church the eighth-grade student may readily think of this year as one of decision, opportunity to make an informed commitment to Christ and unite with the church.

2. Objectives

First semester: (a) To appreciate church history and something of the history of doctrine; (b) to realize the significance of the self in relation to the contributions to Christianity of men like Martin Luther, Roger Williams, William Penn; (c) to grasp the connection that the local church and its denomination has with the main stream of Christian faith. Second semester: (a) To respond to the Christ of the church and the gospels and commit the self to God revealed in Christ; (*b*) to unite with the church.

3. *Content*

As in the seventh grade, so now the teacher will seek to guide this older group in study and fellowship, enabling the young people not only to learn about the church but to experience it as they prepare themselves for full membership in Christian community. Teaching by question and answer, discussion and worship should alternate with relevant dramatic and handwork activities. If the teacher can locate a copy of Convis' book (out of print), certain of the practices in it can be adapted to making the individual's commitment an impressive and lasting experience. In cases of students newly entered upon the curriculum of church education, joining the church or confirmation should be delayed at least for a year so that they can be coached in back work.

BOOKS FOR THE FIRST SEMESTER

For the Teacher

  A History of Christianity, by Kenneth Scott Latourette. Harper & Brothers, 1953.

For the Student

  The Church of Our Fathers, by Roland H. Bainton. The Westminster Press, 1941.

  Martin Luther, by Harry Emerson Fosdick. Landmark Book. Random House, Inc., 1956.

  Lone Journey: The Life of Roger Williams, by Jeanette Eaton. Harcourt, Brace and Company, Inc., 1944.

Penn, by Elizabeth Janet Gray. The Viking Press, Inc., 1938.

Let's Play a Story, by Elizabeth Allstrom. Friendship Press, 1957.

Make It Yourself! Handicraft for Boys and Girls, by Bernice Wells Carlson. Abingdon Press, 1950.

BOOKS FOR THE SECOND SEMESTER

FOR THE TEACHER

Eyes of Faith, by Paul S. Minear. The Westminster Press, 1946.

Adventuring Into the Church, by L. A. Convis. Harper & Brothers, 1951.

FOR THE STUDENT

I Believe: A Christian Faith for Youth, by Nevin C. Harner. Christian Education Press, 1950.

To Know and Believe, by John Wallace Suter. The Seabury Press, Inc., 1958.

Denominational church membership manuals

4. *Evaluation*

The Church Class Report is used to evaluate the work of the student, but the teacher and the class will understand that knowledge is not the main determinant of whether or not one is received into the church. However, given opportunity to have followed this curriculum since the fifth or sixth grade, the student can probably qualify as a knowledgeable communicant.

Grade 9
First Semester: PAUL'S MISSION
Second Semester: MISSIONS TODAY

1. *Characteristics and Needs*

Dr. Ruth Strang finds that " in the ninth grade . . . the large majority of girls will have attained biological maturity; a smaller proportion of the boys will have reached maturity; about a third of the boys will be passing through puberty; and a few will still be children." [42] Teachers, therefore, are dealing with a mixed congregation! There is the womanly girl craving attention from high school or still older males; the rare fourteen-year-old boy whose sexual and social development matches hers; and there is the little boy or girl lost to the emotional pace of the class group. On the other hand, Robert J. Havighurst says: " The brain and nervous system reach adult size at about the age of fourteen. There probably is a further maturation after this age, with chemical changes and growth on a microscopic scale. However, it seems safe to say that the biological basis for adult mentality is present by the age of fourteen." [43] A comparison between the usual kind of teaching and learning carried on at public school with that in the church strengthens the argument for the latter's demanding more rigorous work — simply because students need and respond best to a challenging job. In many respects, if a teacher is to err on one side or the other, it is better to err on the side of expecting too much from the mind of the fourteen-year-old, this rapidly emerging adult whose intellectual and spiritual capacity equip him to respond to the call for Christian living. It is not necessary for the church to surrender the youth to what Prof. P. A. Sorokin, of Harvard, has called " our sensate culture "; but the adolescent's Christian idealism needs direction afforded by the high goal of a personal mission for Christ. In class, in regular congregational worship, and to an ever-expanding extent in the life of the fellowship as a whole, the ninth-grader basically *wants* this year to be one of advance. He does not want to be lost to the church.

2. *Objectives*

First semester: (*a*) To know the life of Paul; (*b*) to read and interpret portions of Paul's letters to the churches; (*c*) to understand the meaning of the church as mission. Second semester: (*a*) To become familiar with current Christian missions; (*b*) to read widely among biographies and other accounts of missionaries and be inspired by them.

3. *Content*

Beyond knowledge in the subjects chosen for the year, opportunity should be given for the class to engage in selected missionary projects and to stimulate the entire local church to do likewise.

BOOKS FOR THE FIRST SEMESTER

For the Teacher

The Interpreter's Bible, Vol. 9. Abingdon Press, 1954.

Paul, by Martin Dibelius, edited and completed by Werner Georg Kümmel; translated by Frank Clarke. The Westminster Press, 1953.

For the Student

Paul for Everyone, by Chester Warren Quimby. The Macmillan Company, 1944.

Letters to Young Churches: A Translation of the New Testament Epistles, by J. B. Phillips. The Macmillan Company, 1947.

BOOKS FOR THE SECOND SEMESTER

FOR THE TEACHER

Missionary Education in Your Church, by Nevin C. Harner and D. D. Baker. Friendship Press, 1950.

The Unfinished Task, by Stephen C. Neill. Alec E. Allenson, Inc., 1957.

The Christian Imperative, by Max Warren. Charles Scribner's Sons, 1955.

FOR THE STUDENT

A Faith for the Nations, by Charles W. Forman. Layman's Theological Library. The Westminster Press, 1957.

They Reach for Life, by John E. Skoglund. Friendship Press, 1955.

Mission: U.S.A., by James W. Hoffman. Friendship Press, 1956.

Sagebrush Surgeon, by Florence Crannel Means. Friendship Press, 1955.

He Wears Orchids: Other Latin American Stories, by Elizabeth Meredith Lee. Friendship Press, 1951.

They Stand Invincible, by Robert Merrill Bartlett. The Thomas Y. Crowell Co., 1959.

Albert Schweitzer: Genius of the Jungle, by Joseph Gollomb. The Vanguard Press, 1949.

4. *Evaluation*

Particular attention is to be paid to the student's special interests and outreach through the church. Although the life in Christian community is given new emphasis, no less attention is due to academic progress and appraisal of it.

SENIOR HIGH
Grade 10
First Semester: PROPHETIC RELIGION
Second Semester: COMPARATIVE RELIGION

1. *Characteristics and Needs*

When *Youth: The Years from Ten to Sixteen* [44] first appeared, a magazine cartoon pictured a school bus driver, parked in front of a school, waiting for his charges, intently reading the book. Youth themselves have been known to reach for the same work, with the quip: " What'm I s'posed to be like now? " Although fifteen-year-olds are entering upon a period of consolidation, there are parents who contend that this is the hard age; and in fact not a few young people just beginning high school find *parents* hard to bring up. For bring them up, youth feel compelled to do; there is so much that oldsters seem not to know, particularly about social graces. In establishing inner authority the adolescent needs to break ties that hold him too close to parents and teachers. Some rush the matter, become defiant, clamor for full adult privileges, including the presumed right — despite the law — to drive the family car. What is indicated is that the adolescent is bent on finding a balance between authority and freedom, which is precisely the problem of every adult. And adolescents seem convinced that parents and teachers are not universally gifted in working out this balance either for or with the young, whose feelings have not caught up with their physical or mental development. The first-year high school student needs the stimulus of significant teaching wherein he is enlisted in open-minded quest after a satisfying and well-grounded way of thinking and acting. It would not be too far off the mark to say that his most basic need is for help in harmonizing worthy outlook and deed. A viewpoint and a code higher than that of the self, that of adult authority, even higher than his cherished peers', fundamentally is what the alert and idealistic high school student desires. Some tenth-graders are already able to depart from standards imposed by their peers, as denoted by ideas held independently, values contrary to those of most of the crowd, and by partial withdrawal from the group in favor of a few close friends or " going steady."

The claims of prophetic religion seem peculiarly appropriate for the first-year high school student. The very lack of adult moral stability in our society and adolescents' own moral and spiritual confusion serve to cause them to seek guidance from prophets, men whose daring and integrity youth may be constrained to emulate. For they are looking for someone who can help them set a worthy direction for life, who can give them vision, a cause to serve. Honest and forthright by nature, youth cannot tolerate hypocrisy: profession minus practice, preachment devoid of integrity. In the prophets of God they discover ideals lived fearlessly. And as their horizon expands they become interested in the teachings of other world faiths. Seldom does a group in midadolescence fail to register desire to investigate the ways and thinking of non-Christian religions.

2. Objectives

First semester: (a) To study the message of the Old Testament prophets and the social and personal situations out of which they came; (b) to enjoy prophetic literature and find affinity with these rebel spirits. Second semester: (*a*) To investigate the teachings of the major faiths in world history; (*b*) to see the year's work in relation to Christianity.

3. *Content*

From the tenth grade on, for the most part, reference books may be the same for teacher and student. The emphasis in the first semester is to be placed on prophecy not as foretelling but forthtelling; in the second semester major attention should be given to mastery of that which is of main importance in the several religions.

BOOKS FOR THE FIRST SEMESTER

The Interpreter's Bible, especially Vols. 5 and 6. Abingdon Press,1956.

A Light to the Nations, by Norman K. Gottwald. Harper & Brothers, 1959.

The Literature of the Old Testament, by Julius A. Bewer. Columbia University Press, 1933.

BOOKS FOR THE SECOND SEMESTER

The World's Religions (revised edition), by Charles S. Braden. Abingdon Press, 1954.

The World's Great Religions, by the Editors of *Life.* Simon and Schuster, Inc., 1957. Or the Special Edition for Young Readers. A Deluxe Golden Book. Simon and Schuster, Inc., 1958.

4. *Evaluation.*

Frequent use is to be made of essays, class reports, and tests. These will affect the standing of the student and consequently what the teacher has to say on the Church Class Report. Reports for this year and the next two count toward work for a diploma. At the same time, due allowance is to be made for high school classes' being also church youth groups.

Grade 11
First Semester: RELIGION IN ART AND MUSIC
Second Semester: SOCIAL ETHICS

1. *Characteristics and Needs*

For a good many years students of human intelligence thought that the growth of brain power was completed by the age of sixteen. Recently, however, there is evidence that " growth in vocabulary and general information continues to a slight degree well into adult years. . . . It seems clear that growth in intelligence is part of the total development of the child. . . . Scholastic success requires motivation or drive as well as capacity and opportunities to learn." [45]

Due to churches' extensive experience with high school students disinclined to study, or even to continue in any way active in the church, the question has to be faced as to whether or not a new departure in education can hold them. Listen to youth talk and one gets the impression that they do not want church programs to be too much like school. Couple this with their marked tendency to reflect American society's penchant for following the easy path in almost all phases of life, and the prospect for rigorous church education fades. Not effort but ease seems to be the dominant desire, yea, demand of people today. Certainly by the eleventh grade or sooner some students will disappear from church education classes. Nonetheless, by sound motivation and uncompromising standards youth's expressed desires and/or sensed needs can be met within the church class that achieves a distinct quality of Christian fellowship. There is justification for the view that, aside from being radical, modern youth lean toward conservatism; they strongly desire to find a place in the adult world and recognize that they must work to gain it. Many a young person continues in school not because of intellectual thirst but because he has been convinced that his future career and economic success depend on academic degrees. This of course is not the highest motivation, but it does signify that effort rather than interest may be the crucial motivating factor in a youth's decision to remain in school. Yet the initial absence of interest is often compensated for by a process of educational involvement that generates interest, and thus motivates continued learning. On this fact church teachers of older high school students can rely.

American high school students have been enriched by music and the arts over the years. Therefore a sizable proportion of church class students will come with pronounced interest in studying the religious as well as the aesthetic nature of art and music, for the adolescent is a lover of beauty as well as truth. And he seeks goodness, regardless of whether or not he says so. Hence, he needs to venture in ethical studies; unless injured beyond restoration, his truth-seeking capacity will not let him rest until he gets things right in his own mind. To know youth is to recognize that they possess inner drives toward goodness, for normally they want to overcome evil.

2. *Objectives*

First semester: (*a*) To appreciate the Judaeo-Christian heritage in the fine arts; (*b*) to enjoy art and sacred music; (*c*) to learn something of the lives of the artists and composers. Second semester: (*a*) To lay a foundation for social ethics from the Christian perspective; (*b*) to survey the problems of peace, world government, race, and economic responsibility; (*c*) to take such group action as may be consistent with Christian ethics and possible for high school students; (*d*) to develop a point of view that unifies beauty, truth, and goodness.

3. *Content*

The stated objectives for the year include subjective appreciation of religion in art and music, and objective study of social and human problems to which the student is led to make an informed response. Suitable group projects on social ethics should be undertaken in the second semester. These involve, for example, ventures in racial and international relations.

BOOKS FOR THE FIRST SEMESTER

Art and Religion (revised edition), by Von Ogden Vogt. The Beacon Press, Inc., 1948.

The Bible in Art: Old Testament. Phaidon Press, London. Distributed by Garden City Books, 1957.

The Old Testament and the Fine Arts, by Cynthia Pearl Maus. Harper & Brothers, 1954.

The Gospel in Art, by Albert E. Bailey. The Pilgrim Press, 1944.

The Gospel in Hymns, by Albert E. Bailey. Charles Scribner's Sons, 1950.

Three Centuries of American Hymnody, by Henry Wilder Foote. Harvard University Press, 1940.

BOOKS FOR THE SECOND SEMESTER

Power for Action, by William A. Spurrier. Charles Scribner's Sons, 1948.

War, Peace, and the Christian Mind, by James Thayer Addison. The Seabury Press, Inc., 1953.

A Fair World for All: The Meaning of the Declaration of Human Rights, by Dorothy Canfield Fisher. McGraw-Hill Book Co., Inc., 1952.

The Racial Problem in Christian Perspective, by Kyle Haselden. Harper & Brothers, 1959.

Religion and Economic Responsibility, by Walter G. Muelder. Charles Scribner's Sons, 1953.

4. *Evaluation*

Recognition is to be given to class as well as to individual accomplishments.

Grade 12
First Semester: INTRODUCTION TO THEOLOGY
Second Semester: CHRISTIAN ETHICS

1. *Characteristics and Needs*

High school seniors are likely to show seriousness of purpose as students and members of society and though a minority are intellectuals, still fewer are moral delinquents. Those who are attracted to the church today may be distressingly few, but their numbers will surely increase in the measure that their guidance and learning experiences prove adequate to meet their needs.

Like a considerable proportion of adult society the youth often knows himself to be in need of fellowship that overcomes a sense of aimlessness and isolation. A product of mass society he may feel that he is less than a member of it; and he wants more than membership, he wants to be united with a more personal sector of society. Perhaps this is chiefly why " going steady " has become the custom, and why so many high school students are marrying. With more and more seniors looking toward college, seeking careers directly dependent on advanced education, and engrossed in earning money to meet their goals, organized religion may exert little appeal. Yet unmet spiritual needs remain. However deeply involved in school and personal interests — finding a college, engaging in athletics, courting, owning a car, and having a good time — the need is still there to know the meaning of existence and to live responsibly with God and man. Though intelligence has matured in the senior student, wisdom has not; hence, vital church guidance and teaching are requisite for checking impulse and freeing the young person to walk humbly and confidently with God. Nor is youth's need fulfilled by this-worldly teaching. Fully aware as he is of the possibility of global extinction, he requires a religious instruction and faith that embrace eternity. In short, he is ready for exposition of a Biblical faith that is in part otherworldly.

2. *Objectives*

First semester: (*a*) To examine man's need today and wherein God meets that need; (*b*) to study introductory theological treatises and formulate one's own doctrinal outlook; (*c*) to become familiar with Biblical eschatology. Second semester: (*a*) To understand the relevance of the Christian ethic to current human behavior and personal problems; (*b*) to read and discuss selected literature in the field; (*c*) to take a considered position on sex, marriage, and career; (*d*) to benefit from realistic guidance at the points of personal needs.

3. *Content*

Subject matter for this and the other high school classes may appear to some to be too advanced. Two things are to be said: first, the teacher will have to be aware of the diversity of ability among the students and use all possible ingenuity to adapt the curriculum to individuals and groupings within the class; second, the better high schools now add certain college courses to their curriculums; hence, some of the same advanced students will be members of church classes.

BOOKS FOR THE FIRST SEMESTER

Man's Need and God's Action, by Reuel H. Howe. The Seabury Press, Inc., 1953.

Pillars of Faith, and *Know Your Faith,* by Nels F. S. Ferré. Harper & Brothers, 1948.

Your God Is Too Small, by J. B. Phillips. The Macmillan Company, 1952.

Trends and Frontiers of Religious Thought, by L. Harold DeWolf. National Methodist Student Movement, 1955.

The Renewal of Hope, by Howard Clark Kee. A Haddam House Book. Association Press, 1959.

Otherworldliness and the New Testament, by Amos Wilder. Harper & Brothers, 1954.

BOOKS FOR THE SECOND SEMESTER

Christian Living, by Stephen F. Bayne, Jr. The Seabury Press, Inc., 1957.

Christian Faith and My Job, by Alexander Miller. Association Press, 1946.

The Human Venture in Sex, Love, and Marriage, by Peter A. Bertocci. Association Press, 1949.

If You Marry Outside Your Faith, by James A. Pike. Harper & Brothers, 1954.

4. *Evaluation*

The Church Class Report will take into account both this year's and previous study. If the student has done creditable work, preferably since the eighth or ninth grade, a diploma will be given. Otherwise, at most, a certificate of attendance may be awarded.

JUNIOR COLLEGE
First Year
First Semester: THE MEANING OF LIFE
Second Semester: BIBLICAL FAITH

1. *Characteristics and Needs*

Students who find themselves in junior colleges may be disappointed people. True, the junior college is rapidly establishing itself as an academically respectable unit in the American educational system, but for the present its student body is likely to be largely composed of persons whose finances or scholastic standing do not permit their going to a preferred four-year college or university. Students attending college in their home community — if among the disappointed ones — will need special understanding as they continue in church education. If their level of aspiration is high, they will do good work both at junior college and the church. But those who lack either ability or educational incentive may require church courses academically inferior to senior high courses. Or they may need less formality in the church classroom than they had as high school students. And they will probably respond better to continued church education if they are given wide choice of elective courses and a full range of social activity. However, exceptionally interested and gifted students will need special assignments, perhaps teaching on a tutorial basis. And another group must be kept in mind: a minority of high school graduates or near graduates, not in college and uninterested in any academic enterprise, may enroll in junior college church classes because they desire social contacts, with a minimum of religious emphasis. Thus college age students enrolled in church classes represent a wider range of ability and interest than younger students. And in view of the fact that about half the more able students of America do not graduate from college, among any group of church youth will be found individuals who possess latent possibility for becoming outstanding students. Predominantly these lack motivation, incentive, " level of aspiration," maturity.

2. *Objectives*

First semester: (a) To find meaning in life; (b) to understand and lift the self's aspirations; (c) to wrestle with Christian realities. Second semester: (a) To return to the Bible and learn to listen to it; (b) to perceive its indispensability for finding truth; (c) to learn to engage in a continuing dialogue with Biblical teaching.

3. *Content*

The instructor will build the course of study in cooperation with the class. Subject to diverse needs and interests, the theme for the first semester may be " The Meaning of Life," and for the second semester, " Biblical Faith." Within these and by use of the recommended books considerable elasticity is allowed.

BOOKS FOR THE FIRST SEMESTER

Guide to the Good Life, by William A. Spurrier. Charles Scribner's Sons, 1955.

Self-understanding Through Psychology and Religion, by Seward Hiltner. Charles Scribner's Sons, 1951.

The Screwtape Letters, by C. S. Lewis. The Macmillan Company, 1943.

Religion and Human Behavior, edited by Simon Doniger. Association Press, 1954.

FOR ADVANCED STUDENTS

Psychotherapy and the Christian View of Man, by David E. Roberts. Charles Scribner's Sons, 1950.

The Courage to Be, by Paul Tillich. Yale University Press, 1952.

The Great Realities, by Samuel H. Miller. Harper & Brothers, 1955.

Life Is Commitment, by J. H. Oldman. Harper & Brothers, 1953.

BOOKS FOR THE SECOND SEMESTER

Understanding the Bible, by Fred J. Denbeaux. Layman's Theological Library. The Westminster Press, 1958.

Rediscovering the Bible, by Bernhard W. Anderson. Association Press, 1951.

Interpreting the New Testament, 1900–1950, and *Introducing New Testament Theology,* by Archibald Hunter. The Westminster Press, 1958 and 1946.

The Holy Scriptures, by Robert C. Dentan and others. The Seabury Press, Inc., 1949.

FOR ADVANCED STUDENTS

Christian Beginnings, by Morton S. Enslin. Harper & Brothers, 1938.

Eyes of Faith, by Paul S. Minear. The Westminster Press, 1946.

New Testament Faith for Today, by Amos Wilder. Harper & Brothers, 1955.

4. *Evaluation*

Students may choose to audit the courses, but if they are working for a junior college church diploma the Church Class Report will be used.

JUNIOR COLLEGE
Second Year
First Semester: PHILOSOPHY OF RELIGION
Second Semester: CHRISTIAN MARRIAGE

1. *Characteristics and Needs*

Less is heard nowadays about the omniscient and skeptical college sophomore. And there is some evidence that unlike youth of previous generations today's college generation is more inclined to accept the existence of God as fact, while yet rejecting much of institutional religion. Less daring, less politically and economically radical, the contemporary student seeks security. Decidedly less prejudiced with respect to race than his parents were at the same age, the student seems to practice tolerance for the sake of tolerance. He shows little faith in world improvement, nor does he feel impelled to throw his energies into building a new order; but he hopes that somehow the race of man won't extinguish itself. Withdrawal into personal concerns marks youth today. Patently they need stirring, stimulus to probe reality and their responsibility for the scheme of things. However, it has to be recognized that most students enlisted for church classes at the junior college level will wish to have their immediate interests met. Instead of studying philosophy of religion they may insist on, at most, a philosophy of life. Instead of a course in Christian world citizenship, they may vote for one on careers. Second-year junior college girls, if not already married, are likely to be engaged and impatient for marriage. And the men are not far behind, for the median age of first marriage for males is 22.8 years, about two years higher than for females. As much as anything else, probably the college student needs guidance in delaying marriage so that he can concentrate on study and preparation for a career. And the second-year junior college person needs special help in planning for further schooling.

2. Objectives

First semester: (a) To put a capstone on education for Christian living; (b) to learn the main problems in philosophy of religion; (c) to gain incentive for continued intellectual and spiritual development. Second semester: (a) To discover wherein the Christian view of sex and marriage departs radically from much current thought and practice; (b) to gain personal guidance with respect to love and marriage; (c) to look beyond personal interests toward social responsibility in today's world.

3. *Content*

As already indicated the instructor may find it wise to fit the work of the first semester to the immediate concerns of the students, but even if the title of the course is " A Philosophy of Life," effort should be made to present the principal parts of the reference books. And if the class has already had adequate study of marriage, some other course may be substituted, preferably one that deals with Christian ethics or Biblical theology in light of the human and world situation.

BOOKS FOR THE FIRST SEMESTER

Education Into Religion, by A. Victor Murray. Harper & Brothers, 1954.

Introduction to the Philosophy of Religion, by Peter A. Bertocci. Prentice-Hall, Inc., 1951.

FOR ADVANCED STUDENTS

Faith, Reason, and Existence: An Introduction to Contemporary Philosophy of Religion, by John A. Hutchinson. Oxford University Press, 1956.

God's Grace and Man's Hope, by Daniel D. Williams. Harper & Brothers, 1949.

Faith and Reason, by Nels F. S. Ferré. Harper & Brothers, 1946.

BOOKS FOR THE SECOND SEMESTER

A Christian Interpretation of Marriage, by Henry A. Bowman. The Westminster Press, 1959.

Human Nature and Christian Marriage, by William P. Wylie. Association Press, 1958.

Venture of Faith: A Guide to Marriage and the Home, by Mary Alice and Harold Blake Walker. Harper & Brothers, 1959.

Sex and Religion Today, edited by Simon Doniger. Association Press, 1953.

The Human Venture in Sex, Love, and Marriage, by Peter A. Bertocci. Association Press, 1949.

A Marriage Manual, by Abraham and Hannah Stone. Simon and Schuster, Inc., 1952.

For Advanced Students

The Mystery of Love and Marriage, by Derrick S. Bailey. Harper & Brothers, 1952.

Love and Conflict: New Patterns in Family Life, by Gibson Winter. Doubleday & Co. Inc., 1958.

4. *Evaluation*

The Church Class Report will take into account the two years of junior-college-level work. For degree candidates whose work has been satisfactory, a diploma will ordinarily be granted — provided the student holds a church high school diploma; but some churches may decide to waive the first diploma requirement.

ADULTS

Elective Courses and Informal Study Groups

At the conclusion of the junior college curriculum, formal church courses give way to informal, ungraded study. It is a good policy to build adult study groups around at least five areas of interest: (1) leadership tasks in the church; (2) parent- and family-life education;

(3) personal and community Christian living; (4) the church universal; and (5) Scripture and revelation.

◈

If before reading this chapter there was doubt that church education lays heavy demands on teacher and pupil, there can be little or none now. It is my hope that the curriculum outline will be acceptable as a working basis and that such modifications as wisdom and experience require will be made by local churches and passed on to others in conference and in print. Perhaps major changes will come first through substitution of certain books, and secondly through rearrangement of topics by age levels. Doubtlessly some books listed for pupils will prove too difficult, and others not sufficiently interesting to intrigue the young. Actually much remains to be done in the writing and publishing of books before they can communicate Christian faith to the respective age levels as satisfactorily as comparable materials in general education communicate their contents. Though the problem of transmitting Christian content is a more difficult one to solve than the teaching of content in other fields, it remains true that religious concepts and knowledge of the Christian faith can be made understandable to growing minds. Certainly in the measure that the substance of books suggested here fails to speak intelligibly to the child and youth, the teacher will have to work all the harder. But it is not to be forgotten that if now we extend the learner, too often in the past we have insulted his intelligence.

Some teachers who set out to use this curriculum outline will wish for detailed manuals and workbooks for the class. Yet the thoroughly competent professional correctly prefers to build his own course and devise lesson plans out of the living situation represented by his pupils. With them he develops workbooks, a creative procedure that reduces likelihood of hobbling the learner to ready-made workbooks.

Lacking here is a list of audio-visual materials, fitted to the several topics and precisely graded. Choosing these teaching aids is a task to keep willing laymen busy from now on! As a starting point they will find helpful what The United Presbyterian Church in the U.S.A. has done along this line. And the periodic listings of the National Council of Churches and the *International Journal of Religious Education* can be used to advantage.

Churches enrolling too few pupils to warrant closely graded classes may combine grades one and two, three and four, and so on, and follow the curriculum topics on a two-year cycle. But this is not so satisfactory as keeping the grades separate, and it further complicates the problem of dealing with the less advanced student. Indeed, this volume has not faced the question of nurturing retarded or nonverbally inclined persons. Rather, the burden of the argument throughout has been on stiff academic and mature interpersonal requirements. This was done deliberately, for authentic Protestantism relies on literacy and mental grasp. Our great weakness is that this aspect of our faith has been handled incompetently. In making this assertion I do not in any sense excuse another major deficiency: that of too little attention to genuine piety represented by those whose faith far exceeds their knowledge or powers of reason. And for my part I eagerly await a treatise by someone dedicated to preparing church teachers for fruitful nurture of these people. And there should be a companion volume on the teaching of competent or even superior minds that do not operate with linguistic facility. For assuredly these are among us in considerable numbers. Ask any schoolman.

It should be clear that church education envisions class fellowships appropriate to each group's developmental level. Thus a climate prevails conducive to a child's social and religious well-being; and out of beneficent inter-personal relations growth emerges; and inhering in this growth-producing atmosphere there is maximum stimulus to learning. Let no one think that church education is a sheer intellectualizing of Christian faith. On the other hand, let no Protestant dismiss as secondary the develop-ment of the mind, the mind with which to love God as truly as with the heart.

Presupposed in this chapter is a good church library. In fact it should be second only to the sanctuary in impor-tance, in favorable location, in appointment, and in con-tents. Its appeal will be enhanced if it is spacious, well lighted, with proper chairs and tables, open shelves con-taining books listed above and many more. Its doors should be open daily, the hours matching the church office hours, with a corps of laymen in charge who enjoy library work. Churches that cannot immediately afford the cost of suf-ficient books and equipment might join with others in the area, share their resources, and locate a library centrally.

◈

Pastor-teachers and supporting laymen, ready to gird up their loins for church education, may think of their venture as the launching of the second phase of the Second Protes-tant Reformation. Is not this the logical and necessary counterpart of the first phase, the revival of Biblical theol-ogy and the church? To this mission the people of the churches, mutual ministers, are invited to give themselves that young and old may grow in grace and in knowledge of the Lord of history.

Notes, Bibliography, and Index

Notes

1. See my articles "Church Education for Today," in *Andover Newton Bulletin*, May, 1959, and "Is the Sunday School Doing the Job?" in *Protestant Church Buildings and Equipment*, November, 1959.

2. Despite what seems almost inevitable, in these pages I try not to use "pastor" and "minister" interchangeably. By "pastor" is meant the designated and thoroughly trained leader of the flock, the shepherd. By "minister" is meant every baptized Christian.

3. A Harper & Brothers publication, unfortunately out of print. This is the story of how one pastor and his students combined high academic achievement with experiences in which God came close through Christian fellowship.

4. See *The Church School*, p. 18.

5. *The Purpose of the Church and Its Ministry*, by H. Richard Niebuhr, p. 31.

6. See his *Stride Toward Freedom*.

7. See Harrison Elliott's *Can Religious Education Be Christian?*

8. *Democracy and Education*, pp. 60, 59.

9. See *Can Religious Education Be Christian?* Ch. XI.

10. *Christian Nurture*, p. 10.

11. *Christian Education Today: A Statement of Basic Philosophy*, p. 16.

12. *The Purpose of the Church and Its Ministry*, p. 83, by H. Richard Niebuhr.

13. *England Before and After Wesley,* by J. Wesley Bready, p. 355.

14. *The Sunday School: Its Origin, Mission, Methods, and Auxiliaries,* p. 68.

15. *Religious Education,* July–August, 1958, p. 378.

16. *School and Society,* November 8, 1958, p. 298.

17. Suggested texts will be listed in Chapter 9.

18. *School and Society,* October 25, 1958, p. 372.

19. *History of American Congregationalism,* by G. G. Atkins and F. L. Fagley, p. 102.

20. See his *Delinquency: Sickness or Sin?*

21. *The Character of Man,* p. 287.

22. See my article " Nurture of the Christian Person," in *The Christian Century,* September 25, 1957. Copyright, 1957, Christian Century Foundation.

23. See *The Rights of Infants,* by Margaret A. Ribble, especially Chapters I, IV, and X.

24. " A Treatise on Christian Liberty," in *Three Treatises,* p. 279.

25. See *Education for Modern Man,* p. 175.

26. See his *Father to the Child.*

27. See Chapter 9 for suggested texts.

28. See *Yearbook of American Churches,* 1959 Edition (edited by Benson Y. Landis, published by the National Council of Churches of Christ in the U.S.A.), especially pp. 287 and 274.

29. *The Church as Employer, Money Raiser, and Investor,* by F. Ernest Johnson and J. Emory Ackerman, pp. 3 and 8.

30. *Ibid.,* p. 10.

31. Although the difference between standard and substandard teaching in general education is not guaranteed by the issuance of a certificate to those adjudged worthy by an accrediting board, on the whole the system merits continuation. This suggests the need for churches to accredit their teachers. It can be done by appropriate revision of ecclesiastical examinations ordinarily required of pastors, thus recognizing the pastor-teacher and the new departure in the Protestant ministry. That such a move would improve both the pastoral and teaching ministry seems assured. With rare exceptions stand-

ards should be upheld strictly.

32. Let it be hoped that the degree, Master of Religious Education, will become the M.A. — Master of Arts in Church Education. Until it does, unfortunately we shall have to continue to refer the M.R.E., as indeed we must speak of the School of Religious Education, until it is given a more appropriate name. I suggest Graduate Church College.

33. *House of Intellect*, Chapters VII and VIII.

34. See *Infant and Child in the Culture Today*, by Arnold Gesell and Frances Ilg. Appendix E. Harper & Brothers, 1943.

35. For example, in *Infant and Child in the Culture Today*.

36. *Growth and Development of the Preadolescent*, by Arthur Witt Blair and William H. Burton, p. 83. Appleton-Century-Crofts, Inc., 1951.

37. *Ibid.*, p. 188.

38. See *The Nature of Prejudice*, by Gordon W. Allport, pp. 43–46. A Doubleday Anchor Book, 1954.

39. *Ibid.*, p. 44.

40. See *Religion and the Growing Mind* (third edition) by Basil Yeaxlee, p. 131. Nisbet and Co., London, 1952.

41. Blair, Arthur W., and Burton, William H., *op. cit.*, p. 163

42. *The Adolescent Views Himself*, p. 222. McGraw-Hill Book Co., Inc., 1957.

43. *Human Development and Education*, p. 136. Longmans, Green Co., Inc., 1953.

44. Arnold Gesell and others. Harper & Brothers, 1956.

45. Ruth Strang, *op. cit.*, pp. 276, 277.

Bibliography

American Council on Education, *The Function of the Public Schools in Dealing with Religion*, 1953.

Atkins, G. G., and Fagley, F. L., *History of American Congregationalism*. The Pilgrim Press, 1942.

Baillie, D. M., *God Was in Christ*. Charles Scribner's Sons, 1955.

Barzun, Jacques, *House of Intellect*. Harper & Brothers, 1959.

Bower, William Clayton, *Character Through Creative Experience*. University of Chicago Press, 1939.

Bready, J. Wesley, *England Before and After Wesley*. Hodder & Stoughton, Ltd., London, 1938.

Bushnell, Horace, *Christian Nurture*. Charles Scribner's Sons, 1864.

Casteel, John L., ed., *Spiritual Renewal Through Personal Groups*. Association Press, 1957.

Coe, George A., *What Is Christian Education?* Charles Scribner's Sons, 1929.

Convis, L. A., *Adventuring Into the Church*. Harper & Brothers, 1951.

Dewey, John, *Democracy and Education*. The Macmillan Company, 1916.

Elliott, Harrison S., *Can Religious Education Be Christian?* The Macmillan Company, 1940.

Grimes, Howard, *The Church Redemptive*. Abingdon Press, 1958.

Hook, Sidney, *Education for Modern Man*. Dial Press, Inc., 1946.

The Interpreter's Bible, Vol. XIII. Abingdon Press, 1952.

Johnson, F. Ernest, and Ackerman, J. Emory, *The Church as Employer, Money Raiser, and Investor.* Harper & Brothers, 1959.

King, Martin Luther, *Stride Toward Freedom.* Harper & Brothers, 1958.

Landis, Benson Y., ed., *Yearbook of American Churches,* 1959 Edition. National Council of the Churches of Christ in the U.S.A.

Luther, Martin, *Three Treatises,* "A Treatise on Christian Liberty." Muhlenberg Press, 1947.

McCann, Richard V., *Delinquency: Sickness or Sin?* Harper & Brothers, 1957.

Miller, Randolph Crump, *Education for Christian Living.* Prentice-Hall, Inc., 1956.

Minear, Paul S., *Eyes of Faith.* The Westminster Press, 1946.

Mounier, Emmanuel, *The Character of Man.* Harper & Brothers, 1956.

Munro, Harry C., *Protestant Nurture.* Prentice-Hall, Inc., 1956.

National Council of Churches, *Christian Education Today: A Statement of Basic Philosophy.* International Council of Religious Education, 1940.

Niebuhr, H. Richard, *The Purpose of the Church and Its Ministry.* Harper & Brothers, 1956.

Niebuhr, H. Richard, Williams, Daniel Day, and Gustafson, James M., *The Advancement of Theological Education.* Harper & Brothers, 1957.

Ostrovsky, Everett S., *Father to the Child.* G. P. Putnam's Sons, 1959.

Ribble, Margaret A., *The Rights of Infants.* Columbia University Press, 1943.

Sherrill, Lewis J., *The Gift of Power.* The Macmillan Company, 1955.

Smart, James D., *The Teaching Ministry of the Church.* The Westminster Press, 1954.

Trumbull, H. Clay, *The Sunday School: Its Origin, Mission, Methods, and Auxiliaries.* John D. Wattles, 1888.

Vieth, Paul H., *The Church School.* Christian Education Press, 1957.

Journals

Blizzard, Samuel W., "The Protestant Parish Minister's Integrating Roles," in *Religious Education*, July–August, 1958.

Cutten, G. B., "College Professor as Teacher," in *School and Society*, October 25, 1958.

Fallaw, Wesner, "Nurture of the Christian Person," in *The Christian Century*, September 25, 1957.

Zeran, F. R., "Inspirational Teacher," in *School and Society*, November 8, 1958.

Index